CONTENTS

KT-228-058

Industry profiles

GREAT FIRST JOB GUIDE

GET IT, KEEP IT, LOVE IT

In association with **doctorjob.com**

First published in Great Britain 2006

A & C Black Publishers Ltd, 38 Soho Square, London W1D 3HB

doctorjob.com
www.acblack.com

A CIP record for this book is available from the British Library.
ISBN-10: 0-7136-7732-5
ISBN-13: 978-0-7136-7732-4

This book is produced using paper that is made from wood grown in managed sustainable forests. It is natural, renewable and recyclable. The logging and manufacturing processes conform to the environmental regulations of the country of origin.

Design by Fiona Pike, Pike Design, Winchester
Typeset by Palimpsest Book Production Limited, Grangemouth, Stirlingshire
Printed in the United Kingdom by Bookmarque, Croydon

INTRODUCTION

With hundreds of thousands of students graduating each year, how can you stand out from the pack? Employers want more and more from their applicants nowadays, and the whole job-hunting lark can seem a daunting prospect. But this book offers you a fresh perspective—it's easy when you know how! The **Great First Job Guide** is the culmination of the knowledge acquired by doctorjob.com throughout the years of their graduate careers website.

So how can a mere book help you to get your dream job? Quite simply by making the whole process much simpler for you. You don't need to pay money to a professional CV writer, or have an uncle on the board of a FTSE 100 company. There are many things you can do while you are at university that make you more employable—some you may already be doing, but haven't realised! First you need to know what type of job you want to do. Easier said than done, one might say, but the first section of this book will show you how. The nitty-gritty of job-hunting is covered in our second section, 'Get that job', which starts on page 73, while the industry profiles from page 205 tell you all you need to know about the main employment sectors. And once that first job is secured, discover how to make the most of it for you and your career in 'Your first day . . . and beyond', from page 143.

The **Great First Job Guide** is a must-have for all students who are serious about their future. As well as pocketing this essential careers guide, make sure to use your university careers service for one-to-one advice and stacks of useful resources. For regular advice, an online community of student job-hunters and all the latest graduate schemes you can apply to, register on doctorjob.com

THANKS

We would like to thank the many graduate recruiters and students who have contributed to the text through their comments.

With particular thanks to:
Katie Simpson and Tim Smedley from GTI Specialist Publishers

Heather Bingham; Laura Brammar for tips on postgraduate study; Nigel Broome for the retail digest; James Edleston for the voluntary work FAQs; Tom Evans for the advertising digest; Annie Kelly for the charities profile; Theodore Kyriacou for advice on banking and investment; Claire McBride for tips on psychometric tests; Angus McKendrick for '5 tips for balancing career choice with financial desperation'; Sue Nickson for part of the civil service profile; Sam Palmer for advice on parents, and securing a good salary/terms; Peter Saunders for the teaching digest; Bob Stead for tips on assessment centres and psychometric tests; Danielle Wrobleski for advice on banking and investment

We'd like to thank KPMG for permission to use extracts of their booklet *A clearly different way to apply – The KPMG guide to online application forms*. Pick up a copy of the booklet from your careers service.

For information on diversity: Madeleine Abdoh; Priya Guha; Nayomi Kasthuriarachchi; Alexa-Maria Rathbone; Kevin Ronan; Mara Yamauchi

For advice on private sector vs public sector: Marina Aldridge; Syreeta Cook; Liz Copeland

For advice on work experience and applications: CITBConstructionSkills recruitment team; Jag Gill; June Kay; Kirsty MacCulloch; Alex Marks; Carolyn Myers; Anna Paynton; Clare Price; Giorgio Rondelli; Philippe Rose; Rebecca Sutton; Sally Whitman; Anna Worsley; Carrie Wyatt

WORK OUT WHAT YOU WANT TO DO

WHAT DO YOU *REALLY* WANT TO DO?

CHOOSE THE RIGHT FIRST JOB

Although people change jobs and indeed career directions frequently these days, it's still important to take care when you choose your first job. Sometimes it can be difficult to know whether you're aiming too low, too high, or at the wrong jobs for the wrong reasons.

As you start out on your job hunt, think about these questions:

✔ What kind of a career have you prepared yourself for?
✔ Are you financially able to hold out for the best job?
✔ How prepared are you to launch a professional job campaign?

So why is my first job so important?

Nowadays, people very rarely work for one company for the whole of their working life; in fact, the average person works for seven or more companies in their lifetime.

When you are looking for your second job, employers will base their evaluation of you on your existing job title and the reputation of the company you are working for. It is extremely difficult to go from a low-level position at an unknown organisation into a much higher position in a well-known organisation. On the other hand, it is much easier to go from a good professional position at a well-known company into a better professional position at an even more successful organisation. All in all,

3

then, a good first job can often make it easier for you to climb the ladder in your chosen field.

Isn't work supposed to be painful? Isn't that why they call it work?

No, work is not supposed to be painful. If you believe that, then you will settle for less and never be completely satisfied. Work is as natural to human beings as breathing. We feel bored, dissatisfied and empty if we cannot contribute to the world in some meaningful way. Freud said that there are two important things in life: work and love.

Don't I have to 'serve my time' first before I can find work I really enjoy?

Certainly you shouldn't expect to jump into the job of your dreams straight out of university. Unless, of course, you started the company! You do need to spend time in a new job learning the ropes and making connections. But don't ever think of it as 'serving my time'. This kind of thinking will encourage you to stay in a job that may not really suit you. You should expect to be excited about going to work each day.

What if I want to work in a non-profit organisation?

Your first job is just as important. There is a hierarchy in the voluntary sector in terms of prestige, power, status, and success, just as there is in the private sector. This hierarchy may not influence career choices so heavily, but it still has an effect. Ideally, you are better off establishing your career by working for a well-known and successful voluntary organisation than by working for a small, idealistic, but unknown and unconnected organisation. If you truly want to have a positive impact on the world (which is most people's motivation for working in a voluntary organisation), you are probably better off if you can do that in an organisation with resources and clout. Read chapter 7 and see the industry profiles at the end of the book for a more detailed look at working in non-profit organisations.

ASK YOURSELF SOME KEY QUESTIONS

The following questions provide food for thought as you take the first steps towards discovering and pursuing your dream job.

> ✔ **What skills and talents do I most value in myself?**
> ✔ **What aspects of my work experience so far have I most enjoyed?**
> ✔ **What is my idea of a 'dream job'?**
> ✔ **What am I willing to sacrifice in order to have a dream job?**

The next major question is 'Do I want to be a specialist or a generalist?' If you have chosen a particular field to pursue (such as biology, engineering, finance, music or nursing) that you are really passionate about, then you probably are a specialist. If, on the other hand, you are interested in eventually becoming an organisational leader or an entrepreneur, you are probably more of a generalist. As a specialist, you would want to choose a first job that allows you in time to progress further in your field. As a generalist, you would want to choose a first job that will offer you opportunities to learn more about other fields, and to develop your leadership abilities.

Now you need to get more specific, and write a 'work purpose statement'. The following exercise is adapted from *Zen and the Art of Making a Living* by Laurence G. Boldt.

> **Complete each of the following sentences:**
> ✔ **The way I want to contribute is . . .**
> ✔ **The people I want to serve are . . .**
> ✔ **The scale I want to work at is . . . (e.g. individual, community, national, global)**

Now combine these sentences into one statement about your work purpose that includes who you want to serve, the way you want to serve them, and the scope of the impact you want to make.

EXPLORE YOUR OPTIONS

It's time to research potential careers.

Make a list of at least ten different roles that would be compatible with your 'Work Purpose Statement'. Now select the three that are most interesting to you.

Now look into the lifestyle associated with each of these jobs. Use the careers service, the Internet, the library and personal contacts if possible to get a better understanding of what it would be like to work in each of these careers. Find out what a typical day is like for someone who does that job so you know what it's *really* like.

Before you make the leap into what you think is your dream job, spend some time thinking about what are absolute necessities in your life and work. Is it essential that you have high earnings, or are you willing to earn less money to do work that is more meaningful to you? Is it essential that you have a steady income, or are you excited about the risk and potential gains of working for a small start-up organisation? Is it essential that you work with people, or are you content to work alone? What things do you think will be absolutely necessary to you in your work? Make a list of five 'must-haves' and five 'nice-to-haves'.

Use companies' websites, brochures and presentations for research.

Assess your financial situation

Work out how long you have to find your first job. If you don't have the financial support to wait for the 'perfect' first job, then decide on your minimum criteria for accepting a position. These criteria could be related to finance, working conditions, or geographic location, for example. At the very least, if you are accepting a job that does not fit your 'work purpose', then be sure that it gives you the time and opportunity to keep looking for a better position.

Don't bow to pressure

All too often, people choose a career path that someone else, such as a parent, teacher, or lecturer thinks is right for them. Often family pressures come into play. If your grandfather and mother were both teachers, you may be expected to follow them in their chosen career path. Resist this pressure if you can, as it doesn't take into account *your* gifts and talents. If you want to do something else entirely, keep plugging away until you find the right job for you.

If your family has links to a family business, it may be that you are expected to join that business. Or maybe your parents will encourage a family friend to take you on. It might seem like an easy solution to finding your first job, but doing this unless you really want to means abdicating all responsibility for yourself and putting the direction of your life and career in someone else's hands. It may be that such an opportunity is for you—in which case, great. Do take time to analyse your motivations, though, so that you know you are making a rational and informed decision.

Beware of a job that is too good to be true, especially if you are being asked to put in your own money, or to work for very low amounts at first. Con men understand the hunger that people have for a dream job, and they can play on that. If you are being offered a job that really seems to fit what you are looking for, make sure that you are going to be paid what you are worth.

Don't be dissuaded from following a dream

Don't miss out on trying to find the kind of work you would really love, because people tell you that you are being impractical, unrealistic, idealistic or selfish, or that the job market is bad. Remember that just because it's never been done before, it doesn't mean that you can't do it; it's amazing what you can achieve if you're determined. You can be incredibly creative and resourceful. It may be that you will have to work harder and take a little longer to move into the career you would really love to have, but it will be worth it in the long run.

7

Bear in mind that the most successful business people and entrepreneurs were frequently told that what they wanted to do was 'impossible'.

If you need time to think about your future then consider short-term or voluntary work.

Think long-term

Don't make the mistake of jumping at the first offer without considering some of the potential pitfalls. It's understandable that people take the first offer they get even if they've applied for several jobs, especially if money is tight and they're itching to move on and start the next part of their life.

Conversely, sometimes people get too attached to their idea of what a 'perfect job' would look like. Beware of being too picky and of passing by opportunities that could turn out to be even better than the job you are looking for. Keep an open mind, but at the same time don't settle for something that doesn't fit your values, or that doesn't really use your most important skills and talents.

Many people think that they just have to look around hard enough until they find their dream job. The truth is that most people who have 'found their calling' have actually created the work that they do. You need to network, make connections, and tell people about your dreams. In doing this you are increasing the chances of finding someone who has just the right piece of information, or just the right connection for you.

If you do get an offer but you're not sure about accepting it, don't be afraid to ask (politely!) for a little time to think it over carefully. Make sure you thank the employer for their offer, give them a date (say two or three days hence) when you'll get back to them, and stick to it. It's never wise to accept or decline a position without a little bit of cooling-off time.

If you are lucky enough to be offered several alternatives when you are looking for your first job, it is tempting to take the one with the best salary. When you are starting your career, this is what seems to make the most sense but it is short-term thinking. If the job does not fit your personality or your sense of purpose in life, you will either be looking for another job very soon, or you will stay and be miserable. It's much better to take a long-term view when you accept your first job. Ask yourself how the job will help you to develop your skills and help you reach your ultimate goal.

FIVE TIPS FOR BALANCING CAREER CHOICE WITH FINANCIAL DESPERATION

1 **Don't skimp on research.** It's worth taking the time and making the effort to search your soul, investigate careers and come up with the 'perfect' job for you. Even if it's something like social work or the media, which could require unpaid work experience to get started, you may be able to think laterally and find an alternative career path. You could exercise your creative or caring skills in, say, teaching, then make a career change. At least you'd have picked up some relevant skills and experience (as well as possibly getting your debts paid off).

2 **Think long term.** Some careers pay badly at the beginning, but go up rapidly and have fabulous long-term prospects. When you're the head of social work for a local authority, earning £75K a year, your student debts are going to look pretty piddling.

3 **Don't look down your nose at temping.** If you're still a student or you've just graduated, why not do some data entry at a local publishing company? It pays just as well as temping elsewhere (unlike the permanent jobs!) and it could be your foot in the door, not to mention useful on the old CV. Temping usually allows the recently graduated to earn a decent wage, gain experience and also take time off for 'proper' job interviews.

4 **Consider postgraduate study . . . cautiously.** In some lucrative careers, such as law, a certain amount of postgraduate study is a necessity. In others, such as environmental work, further study could give you the edge over the competition. The drawback is of course that funding it probably means further debt. Research is crucial here. Investigate all possible sources of funding and evaluate your chances realistically, even if that

means asking admissions tutors difficult questions about employment rates after their courses. The stakes are high, so don't take uncalculated risks.

4 **Don't bow to parental pressure.** If your parents are amongst your creditors, they may put even more pressure on you to find a 'good job'. But do remember that their perception of graduate careers is probably about thirty years out of date and, worse, that they probably have a subconscious desire for you to fulfil their lost ambitions. Try to turn their parental concern towards positive and practical measures, like introducing you to all their friends with interesting jobs and helping you to build a network. That way, they're likely to be paid back sooner rather than later—both emotionally and financially.

WHERE NEXT?

The Job Hunters Bible: **www.jobhuntersbible.com**
Bolles, Richard. *What Color is Your Parachute?* Berkeley, California: Ten Speed Press, updated annually.

WORKING OUT YOUR STRENGTHS

BEGIN WITH THE END IN MIND

Most of us tend to think too narrowly about our strengths and the skills we have to offer, and end up underselling ourselves when we are looking for a job or promotion.

Here is a step-by-step guide to examining your life and work experiences, so that you can assess which of the many skills you have are the most marketable in order to 'sell' yourself more effectively when you apply for that ideal job.

As you read this, think about these questions:

✔ What are my personal and career goals?
✔ What educational, work and leisure experiences have I had that will help me to reach these goals?
✔ Do I have a realistic idea of the match between my skills and my career goal?

If you have worked through the stages in the previous chapter, you should be well on your way to answering these crucial questions.

It takes a lot of time and energy to identify your strengths and marketable skills. It is not an easy task, but it is one of the most important you can undertake. Carefully going through this process will help you to know yourself better, to plan your job campaign and to target the best potential employers. It will also give you a strong sense of confidence in what you have to offer.

Remember that it's never a waste of time to think about what you've done, what you're doing now, and what you want to do next. Working out or just re-examining your career objective will mean that you can home in on the best skills you have and transfer those to job applications that really do you justice. Additionally, it will help you to identify any skills that you need to acquire in order to achieve your objective.

It's never a good idea to jump straight into applying for jobs without working out your strengths. You may think that you already know all your skills, but this exercise often produces some surprising results that can help you market yourself better. Sometimes it even shows you that you may be looking at the wrong career. If this is the case, you can move your ambitions towards something that suits you better.

WRITE A BRIEF BIOGRAPHY

Now that you've spent some time thinking forward to where you want to be in the future, sit down and write a three- to five-page history of where you've been and what you've learned so far in your life.

As you write about each experience, describe what you enjoyed and what you didn't enjoy, and what you accomplished. What are you most proud of? Then describe what you did when you were not studying or working, and how you felt about those activities. Make sure that there are at least seven key events in your biography. Think about:

- ✔ significant events when you were growing up
- ✔ educational achievements
- ✔ important life experiences, such as travelling
- ✔ a summary of your work experiences

REVIEW YOUR EXPERIENCES

Education

Use these questions to work out some of your skills and interests:

- ✔ Which teachers or lecturers did I like best and why?
- ✔ Which teachers or lecturers did I like least and why?
- ✔ Which subjects did I like best and why?
- ✔ Which subjects did I like least and why?
- ✔ In which subjects did I get the best marks and why?
- ✔ In which subjects did I get the worst marks and why?
- ✔ Have I done any further studies outside full-time education? What motivated me?
- ✔ If I've recently decided to gain a new qualification or take up a new hobby, what motivated me to do that?

Take some time to think about your answers and how they might relate to your job search and your skills. For example, if you found that, on reflection, you enjoyed classes or seminars that forced you to think on your feet or present your thoughts to large groups, you could be the type of person to flourish in a sales role. Whatever your findings, try to draw out five key skills, motivations, or areas of knowledge that you might like to use in your career.

Work

Now think about your work experiences so far (this may be temping, bar work, or even babysitting). Look back at each of the jobs you've had and ask yourself:

- ✔ Which was my favourite job and why?
- ✔ Which was my least favourite job and why?
- ✔ Would I do any of these jobs even if I didn't get paid? Why?
- ✔ Did any of the jobs really challenge me and help me to develop personally and professionally? How?

Now identify five key skills or knowledge areas that you might like to use in your career.

Leisure

What do you really enjoy doing with your free time (whether in the evenings, at the weekends or during the holidays)? Think about:

- ✔ What marketable skills have you developed from a hobby? For example, if you enjoy getting involved in theatre productions, do you hanker after the main part? Or are you a behind-the-scenes person; just as important, but gaining organisational skills?
- ✔ What skills have you developed from other leisure activities? For example, if you play sport regularly, have you found that you enjoy leading or motivating others as captain or vice-captain of your team?
- ✔ Is there something you do for fun that you always dreamed of getting paid for? For example, if you enjoy making cards to send to friends and family, would you love to design for a living?
- ✔ What skills have you developed from your travels? For example, have you learnt a new language or lived abroad for a period of time?

Again, identify the five most marketable skills you've gained from your leisure activity assessment.

Other areas of your life

Even stressful experiences can provide us with helpful perspectives on life; think back over things that have happened to you and how they've shaped your life and your goals.

For example, if you've done any voluntary work, have you gained trans-ferable skills or qualifications from that?

List your achievements

Now re-read what you have written and list at least ten major achieve-ments in your life. It doesn't matter if they're not work-related. Then rank your achievements in order, from '1', as the most important achievement, to '10', the least important.

PUT EVERYTHING TOGETHER

Create a final 'skills inventory'

A 'skills inventory' gathers together all the key points you've discovered in the steps above. To compile your inventory:

1   List all your skills that are related to management. You may not be applying for a managerial role just yet, but it's never too early to show leadership skills. Management-related tasks can include:
    - ✔   managing projects
    - ✔   solving problems
    - ✔   managing budgets
    - ✔   planning, organising, and presenting work
2   List the times you have most successfully researched and prepared essays or presentations, summarised research, and so on.
3   List all your technical skills, such as knowledge of computer programs. Include any specialised knowledge or skills that you haven't already mentioned.
4   List all your interpersonal skills. Although these can be hard to define, they are very important and can often make or break a job application. Interpersonal skills can include:
    - ✔   being able to communicate clearly and easily
    - ✔   making things happen
    - ✔   helping and instructing more junior staff
    - ✔   getting people to agree to compromise
    - ✔   negotiating
    - ✔   team building
5   Create a category of 'Other Skills' for any that don't fit into the above categories. Often, these skills are something unique that you have to offer, making you potentially more attractive than other candidates.

Compare the list with your career goals

By now you should have a good list of your strengths and marketable skills. Go back through your list and tick those skills that most closely match your career goals. From these ticked items, choose the ten that you think are most marketable. Write a sentence to say how you have actually used each skill from your list of the top ten.

Don't be put off by an industry's stereotype.

Do a reality check

Now go through your network of friends and family, and try to find someone who is doing the job that you would like to have. Ask them to review your list of skills and say if they match the kind of position you would like. If they don't think there is a match, ask what skills you need to gain. Or you may wish to ask what kind of a job would be a better match for someone with your skills.

Alternatively, ask someone close to you to you to review your skills and to see if you have left anything out. Try to find someone who you know will tell you the truth and offer constructive advice rather than blanket approval—while that's great to hear, it won't be helpful if it's not true.

The next step

Finally, you need to turn your list of marketable skills into key information on your application forms, in your covering letters, and on your CV! Read pp.75–97 for help on producing winning CVs, covering letters and application forms.

WHERE NEXT?

The CV-index directory: **www.cvindex.com**

GetMyOnlineCV.com: **www.getmyonlinecv.com**

Guardian Jobs: **jobs.guardian.co.uk/careerscentre**

Identify your skills: **doctorjob.com/jobhuntingessentials**

MAKING THE MOST OF CAREERS SERVICES

ARE YOU BEING SERVED?

For the first year or so of university, the last thing on your mind is your career. There's some serious partying to get in before you contemplate The Rest Of Your Life.

But it's never too early to pay a visit to your friendly university careers service. It's chock-full of handy information about all kinds of careers-related stuff you can do outside the lecture theatre.

Did you realise a visit to your careers service could fix you up with a handy part-time job? Or maybe even open your eyes to a world of holiday opportunities?

Ask the experts

Let's start with a myth: nobody needs a university careers service nowadays. You can get loads of information from the internet, and you can even apply online, so there's no need to get off your bottom and visit your careers service. That is simply not true. The internet definitely is a valuable job-hunting tool, but your careers service offers things that just aren't available online. Read on to discover just a few of the wonderful things your careers service may offer.

✔ **Jobs bulletins.** Once you've registered with your careers service you should get free updates just bursting with available jobs, sent either by post or by e-mail every week or fortnight. Not all organisations advertise their vacancies online, so your careers service may have information about jobs that will never pop up on a computer screen. The jobs bulletin may also include local employers who don't advertise anywhere else.

✔ **A nifty noticeboard.** Even if you get a regular vacancy bulletin, it's worth nipping in occasionally to see what nuggets your careers advisers have posted up, such as ads from the national press, local opportunities and campus careers events.

✔ **Recruitment fairs.** These are brilliant opportunities to check out lots of employers at once. Your careers service may host specialised events as well as larger fairs covering all job sectors. Some simply convey information, while others are recruitment fairs and should be treated like first interviews. Some mix employers with alumni who come back to talk about their experiences of job seeking and work in a particular field. It's guaranteed that any employer who turns up is interested in people studying at your university.

✔ **Employer events.** Big graduate employers try to attract top graduates by holding presentations and workshops, which are coordinated by—you've guessed it—your careers service. Events come in many forms, from an applications workshop or a mini-course on marketing to a soirée at a posh hotel. This is your chance to find out if they're worth applying to and—if they are—to make a good impression. If you don't register at your careers service you risk not knowing about the event and not being able to sign up, as places are often limited.

✔ **Files on graduate employers.** If you've made a shortlist of employers, you can probably read all about them in the careers service's files. If this sounds a bit sinister or a tad low-tech, you're missing the point. The file may indeed contain yellowing press cuttings about dastardly goings on at company X, but it should also have the recruitment brochure, the annual report, feedback from alumni employed by X, interview notes from previous candidates and many other useful nuggets.

✔ **Careers advisers.** If you've got a question about anything careers-related, just go down to your careers centre and ask. Careers advisers are there to help you, and usually have 'quick query' or 'drop in' sessions where you can get your CV checked or seek basic advice. For more detailed discussions you can book a longer appointment. Advisers often specialise in a certain sector, so they are genuinely likely to know something about employers in that area.

✔ **Careers directories and publications.** There are probably piles of publications bursting with job ads conveniently placed and just waiting for you to take them away. Some of the more popular ones run out quickly, so do check the reference section and 'occupational' files too. Bigger services may have a *Careers Service Guide*, or something similar, with directory listings of employers interested in students from your institution. That's the great thing: any employer in the directory is interested in you, simply by virtue of the university you go to.

✔ **Recruitment brochures and application forms.** A lot of these are online now, of course, but it can be nice to have a paper copy, and your careers service will have a good supply. That way you won't have to remember the Web address, you can read it at your leisure, and you can make notes or doodle in the margins.

✔ **Careers library.** The library will have information on immediate vacancies in the local area as well as local newspapers containing jobs sections. You'll also find information on holiday placements in the UK and overseas, student membership of professional bodies and advice on applications and interviews. You may even have found *this* book in your careers library!

✔ **Details of events.** In addition to recruitment fairs and employer events (see above), careers services organise events relating to a wide variety of subjects, including overseas work placement organisations, careers education courses, work experience opportunities and further study.

Gissa (part-time) job

As well as earning valuable cash, part-time work can boost your employment prospects. It will open your eyes to Life in the Real World and can be used as evidence of your ability to deal with customers, handle cash and work in a team.

Find out if your careers service houses a job shop (if not there might be one in your students' union) and what other information they hold on local employers. This can range from directories of organisations to local papers and immediate vacancy notices.

Most careers services will still provide information and advice three years after you've graduated.

Make the most of university life

Never again will you have so much free time at your disposal. For some of you that spare time will be taken up with sporting, theatrical or musical interests you've already developed. For many more, university means a chance to get involved in something new. Why not find out about activities the careers service recommends? Working as a teacher's assistant in a local secondary school or spending Saturdays clearing out derelict canals isn't for everyone, but how do you know until you try?

Draw up a timetable of applications for your final year.

Fill those long summer holidays

A visit to the careers service will reveal loads of schemes open to students wanting to make the most of their time, whether they're interested in rescuing Costa Rican turtles, helping disadvantaged city kids or getting work experience with an investment bank. If nothing else, it will make your parents glow with pride.

Careers services are open during term time and sometimes with restricted hours during holidays. Most services invite you to register to receive regular e-mail updates. The staff are used to all kinds of weird and wonderful requests, so don't be shy. If you can't get to your careers service, visit its website or use the careers guidance software on your university computers to access databases of local employers and university alumni.

So what are you waiting for? Now that you know how wonderful your careers service is, get down there and check it out!

WHERE NEXT?

gradireland.com (for links to careers services in Ireland and Northern Ireland): **www.gradireland.com/advice**
NUS careers service (follow the links to your institution's careers service): **www.nusonline.co.uk/info/careers**

GETTING THE BEST
FROM YOUR
WORK EXPERIENCE

ARE YOU EXPERIENCED?

With so many students graduating every year it takes more than just your academic ability to impress employers. Work experience provides an excellent opportunity to prove you have self-motivation as well as enabling you to earn some extra cash.

You'll enhance your CV, but you'll also get an insider's view of an industry, be given the chance to network and make contacts who could help you to secure a permanent position after you graduate. Even if your work experience isn't related to your future career you will have developed skills that are essential in most jobs and, more importantly, you'll have proved that you didn't just sit on your backside all holiday playing on your Xbox.

Without work experience on your CV, employers will struggle to believe you have the necessary skills and capabilities to work for them. Academic qualifications are still vitally important, but in the tough world of graduate recruitment you need to prove you are capable and committed outside the lecture theatre as well.

All the reasons for doing work experience amount to one thing: it's what recruiters want.

However, if you undertake work experience just so that you can tick a box on an application form, then you're missing the point. Recruiters look for well-rounded individuals and, in order to find out what sort of person you are, they need to know what experiences you've had in life.

KNOW YOUR OPTIONS

You may not know a sandwich course from a sandwich filling, or think that work shadowing sounds like a mime act, but panic not—by reading this book you've made a great start in finding the right work experience and employer for you. It's helpful to know what's on offer . . .

✔ **Gap year.** Also known as a year out, students often take a gap year before starting University or immediately after they have graduated. Knowledge and experience of living and working in other countries can be both broadening and confidence-building as well as very enjoyable. See chapter 6 (from p.37) for a more detailed look at gap years.

✔ **Placements** are becoming a necessary part of vocational degrees. Organisations in sectors such as engineering and construction often offer formal, structured work experience over the summer break. You'll be helped to secure a place by a placement tutor.

✔ **Internships.** For some, these are the *crème de la crème* of work experience opportunities—usually undertaken in the summer before your final year, it's the big boys of the recruitment world who offer internships, and they demand a high calibre of applicant.

70% of people who undertake year- or summer-long internships or placements receive a graduate job offer from the company. Source: University of Manchester

✔ **Sandwich courses** are a year of work between your first two years and your final year at university. Also known as industrial placements, these are built into your degree course and you will be paid a reasonable wage. They are most commonly an element of engineering, language and science courses. You will be expected to assume the role of a regular employee and given responsibilities and duties to match. This may sound intimidating but large organisations often have mentoring schemes in place to ensure that you receive all of the support necessary to perform at the required level. Universities should have a tutor to help you to arrange your year in industry. Be proactive in securing a place with the right employer to ensure you get the most out of your year.

✔ **Holiday placements** will usually be paid and structured to fit to your university holiday dates, running between two and eight weeks. One of these on your CV will help to show that you have a good level of commitment to the industry and to developing your skills.

90% of UK-based students work during the long summer break. Source: NASES

✔ **Voluntary work** can be anything from mending fences in a national park, to helping out a local charity, saving the mountain tigers of Ecuador or simply working for free at a fashion magazine. In the case of charities and conservation work, your passion and commitment will impress potential employers. You may even be able to help out in a role that's close to your chosen career route, such as finance, IT or press relations. Volunteering can also be the way into media, such as TV, PR or magazines, where starting from the bottom can often be the only way in. See chapter 7 (p.45) and the industry profiles at the back of the book for a more detailed look at the benefits of volunteering and charity work.

75% of employers state a preference for applicants with voluntary work experience. Source: Tearfund survey

✔ **Part-time and casual work** while at university or over the holidays can help to fund your degree while also gaining important skills. Whether it's working in a bar or office temping, you can use your experiences to illustrate anything from difficult situations overcome, to customer service skills, teamwork and business acumen.

✔ **Work shadowing** involves you closely observing a professional in their daily working life, for a period usually ranging from a day up to one week, to see if their job interests you. You will get first-hand experience of time pressures and workloads.

✔ **Work tasters** are very short placements offered by some organisations, sometimes in conjunction with careers services, to give you an insight into a job role or department.

✔ **International exchanges** are reciprocal arrangements between similar institutions, usually for languages students, where a period of time is spent overseas.

✔ **Open days** provide you with the opportunity to get a taste of a particular type of work or company without making a commitment. They include presentations, business games and the chance to talk with recent graduates.

10 SKILLS EMPLOYERS LOVE

1   Communication
2   Teamwork
3   Enthusiasm, drive and motivation
4   Planning, organisation and time management
5   Interpersonal skills
6   Commercial awareness
7   Flexibility and adaptability
8   Initiative
9   Independence
10 Problem solving

WORK EXPERIENCE APPLICATIONS: WHY THEM AND WHY YOU?

As the most valuable work experience placements are often the most competitive, you will need to approach your application in the same way as you would a 'normal' job application.

Make sure your application is tailored towards the specific organisation and the work experience they offer. In recruiting students for their placement scheme, employers are usually looking for potential future employees. In some organisations the recruitment and selection of placement students is given as much attention as the recruitment of permanent staff. Your covering letter and CV are vitally important; read the relevant chapters for advice on these.

✔ **Applying 'on spec'.** Speculative applications can be a way into organisations that don't advertise work experience. Try to think about what the company would gain from offering you a placement and then articulate this to them. Again, you need to tailor your application in order to make it stand out. Find the name for whoever deals with such queries, such as the HR manager—look on the website or make a quick phone call.

✔ **Application forms.** A formal work experience scheme will often have an application form to go with it. These are designed to extract the right amount of information needed to select or reject you. The better systems also give you rapid feedback on your application, your strengths and weaknesses and your chances of getting a job with them. Look at chapter 13 (from p.89) for more in-depth guidance.

Remember that if you are really enthusiastic about gaining experience with a particular organisation, your enthusiasm will be infectious and flattering. But it's also important to learn how to handle rejection. You should see a 'no' as an opportunity to ask for feedback that could help you to improve your chances in the future.

START SMALL FOR BIG RESULTS

When you first start looking for work experience you can be forgiven for feeling daunted.

Scare stories fly around, such as, 'employers only take people with ten years of relevant internships and two firsts from Oxford'. But the truth is that you can gain many of the skills and capabilities you need from jobs that are quite modest in scope. The jobs you do to help finance yourself through university—such as bar work, shop assistant or temping—can be of real benefit. Fitting working around your studies also shows dedication, time management, commitment and a 'get-up-and-go' attitude.

Can bar work really help?

Of course! You can pick up such transferable skills as teamworking, customer service, problem solving, creative thinking and numeracy from any part-time job. The most important thing for employers is that they have applicants who understand the demands of a working environment, and have some experience of the 'real world' outside academia.

Finding part-time work

There are many ways to find part-time and casual work. Your careers service will have links with local employers and can help you to find work during term time—some services have a job shop for this purpose, as do many student unions. Check out your union and career service websites for details of online job boards. Or you can apply 'on spec' to any place of work—the best way to do this is to print off your CV, dress smartly and go in and ask.

Relevant experience with SMEs

Once you have some part-time work under your belt, and some spare cash in the bank, it might be time to get some work experience that's directly relevant to a career path that interests you. Small- to medium-sized companies (SMEs) can offer unique opportunities to build and develop your skills, a chance to influence decision making and be given real responsibilities. Your careers service and job shop should be your first port of call—remember to ask specifically about any regional schemes or initiatives which may run in your area. There are structured schemes that can help you to find a suitable SME placement, such as the Shell STEP scheme, which runs a UK-wide programme that helps second year and penultimate year students to find project-based placements with SMEs.

FOUR TIPS FOR MAKING THE MOST OF YOUR SME PLACEMENT

1 Listen and learn from your colleagues and managers.
2 Don't hold back from making your own suggestions and sharing your ideas.
3 Keep a record of all the projects you've been involved with, the contributions you've made and skills you've picked up.
4 Most importantly, enjoy it!

THINK BIG

If you want your own project, real responsibility and some enviable contacts, then try work experience with one of the big players.

In a graduate market rife with similarly qualified candidates an internship at a large organisation can be the opportunity you need to demonstrate your talents. Because they have unrivalled resources, such placements allow you to see developments at the cutting edge of the industry and work on high-profile projects. There is also the added incentive that large recruiters can offer many of their graduate-level positions to previous interns.

Large recruiters are particularly adept at making the most of the time available during university holidays. 'Our summer vacation programme is seven weeks long—after a week of induction you'll be fully equipped to join your department,' says a senior manager in graduate recruitment at Deloitte. 'They will know well in advance that you'll be joining and have scheduled you real client work for the whole six weeks. During this time you can expect to be treated exactly the same as a new graduate joiner.' To really maximise your experience make sure that you ask for feedback from your colleagues and mentors so that you can see what you are doing well and where you might need to improve.

And finally . . .

The most important thing to consider when organising your placement is what type of experience you want. If you fancy a brief taster of a variety of different roles then consider applying for several short placements at different employers. Many offer summer, Easter and Christmas placements as standard, but there are also opportunities year round, particularly at large recruiters where extra people are always of use. If you want a comprehensive experience and an insight into the work of a large multinational, then check the big employers' websites for vacancies. Whether you end up at a tiny organisation or as an integral part of a new department at one of the big blue-chip employers, do your research to make sure that your placement suits you.

FOUR TIPS FOR MAKING YOUR WORK EXPERIENCE WORK FOR YOU

1   Ask lots of intelligent questions to raise your awareness.
2   Keep a diary of the work you carry out, any computer software packages you use, training received, etc.
3   Ask people you meet for their contact details and other contacts they feel would be helpful for you.
4   Don't wait to be told what to do next—use your initiative.

SELL YOUR EXPERIENCE TO EMPLOYERS

Don't forget that, on paper, the majority of applicants are all much of a muchness.

What will set you apart from the others is the way that you answer the competency or additional questions the recruiter may ask. It's worth spending some time thinking about your answers to make sure that you are selling yourself. So let's find out how . . .

Keep a diary of your experience

There's no need to go to Bridget Jones proportions but simply list all the new skills you pick up, any training you receive, difficult situations overcome, teamwork examples, recognised contributions and so on. You should make the most of the transferable skills you have gained, rather than focusing on the actual routine tasks completed. This way you can be specific about your involvement and won't have to rely on memory to remember important details.

Be specific

Use specific examples such as scheduling a project from start to finish and the value it added to the company. The bottom line is that employers want to know that you are suitable for the job and the company. Explain how things you learned on your placement, such as time management, diplomacy and communication skills, organisation and leadership, could be transferred into your new position.

If you've done an unusual form of work experience, make sure you focus on the uniqueness of the experience and the transferable skills you picked up. Volunteering or travel can tell employers a lot about a person and may set you apart from other applicants.

Examples of creativity and initiative

The buzzwords of modern graduate recruitment are 'creativity' and 'initiative'. How you initially secured your work experience placement could be evidence of initiative; if you manage to secure a placement which was not advertised, you can use that success to demonstrate your interpersonal skills and ability to 'think outside the box'. Taking part in a formal summer vacation programme at an early stage in your career can also display these skills.

Business awareness

A common complaint from employers is that students lack business awareness. Your work experience should have given you an understanding of how a business works. Can you demonstrate that you developed an overview of the dynamics of a work environment, of the aims of a business and of how the different functions such as production, sales, marketing and human resources all relate? The more specific you can be, the better.

Follow the STAR

When asked to give examples from your work experience, covering any skill or competency, it can be very useful to use the STAR method—situation, task, action, result.

Describe a specific *situation* that occurred while on your placement, then the *tasks* you were given, the *action* you decided to take and finally the *result* of those actions.

This is a useful way of being concise and to the point in application forms, and also helps to stop you from waffling at interview. This is only a basic structure, but if you ensure that you hit on these four main points (in order) then you will really enhance your answers.

You can also finish by saying what you learnt from the experience, and how it would help you in the job for which you are applying. The best way to sell yourself is to be enthusiastic. Be positive about your work experience and how you want to develop what you learned as a graduate recruit, and you'll be an outstanding applicant!

FAQS

How can I impress during my internship?

Use your initiative to take control of your own development. Demonstrate a 'can-do' attitude: it will broaden your horizons, increase your confidence, and show people what you are capable of.

Does work experience have to be in the same sector to secure future employment?

Generally when employers take on a graduate they understand that they will be a bit of a 'blank canvas'. Relevant experience can be an advantage, particularly in competitive arenas such as the media where you need to be able to talk the language from day one, but having a broad interest in a number of areas, including a variety of work experience, gives the impression of a well-rounded individual.

WHERE NEXT?

Find out more from doctorjob: **doctorjob.com/workexperience**
goWales (for opportunities in Wales): **www.gowales.co.uk**
Shell STEP scheme (a UK-wide programme offering students work experience placements): **www.step.org.uk**

WORKING DURING YOUR HOLIDAYS

WORK OUT WHY YOU SHOULD SPEND YOUR SUMMER AT WORK

Never again will you have three whole, sun-kissed months in which to sunbathe, synchronise your sleep cycle with that of the Big Brother *housemates and generally just do nothing at all.*

If this sounds anything like your plans for the summer, you're probably (a) rather in need of a life, and (b) part of a small minority. So why are so many people swapping the sofa for the supermarket till?

90% of UK-based students do some form of work during the holidays Source: NUS

Graduate careers with attitude

For most people the motivator is, of course, money; for many students, not getting a job during the summer holiday is just not an option any more. But this is far from the only reason to find work. For starters, it'll stop you going insane with boredom watching Andy Murray lumbering after the ball all summer. But most important by far are the skills you'll pick up. The most common fault that recruiters find with graduates is their ineptitude at the things that can only really be practised in the workplace, such as commercial awareness or customer service. With the right atttude, you can boost your CV with useful, transferable, work-related skills that will have recruiters positively salivating—it's all about how you transfer the experience to paper afterwards.

I'm a student . . . get me a job!

So how do you go about finding summer work? Placement agencies, such as STEP, arrange paid placements on short-term projects with small to medium-sized companies (known in the trade as SMEs) for penultimate year students. There are several regional schemes that link students seeking summer work with employers looking for short-term, undergrad talent. Cymru Prosper Wales organises ten-week placements in Wales, while Graduate Advantage arranges work placements for students in the West Midlands. The great thing about working for a smaller organisation is that you're more likely to be handed unexpected responsibilities, which are great for those application form questions that follow the format: 'describe a time when you led a team/solved a problem/fought wolves with your bare hands'.

Keeping it casual

It's easy to think of work experience as something that has to be 'worthwhile'. But not everyone volunteers, goes abroad or rescues a small company from bankruptcy during their break. No matter how casual the work is, any experience is beneficial as long as you've made the most of it. Take the classic example of stacking shelves—you might see not much more than a mind-numbing job and 500 tins of beans. A careers adviser would see teamwork, customer service and the ability to stay motivated during repetitive tasks. Basically, it's not what you do, but how you do it. Simple things, like turning up on time, taking the initiative and going out of your way to help others, can't fail to impress and will come across on your references. There are heaps of ways to turn any kind of work to your advantage—see 'How to milk it' below.

Just remember, the fact that any job can be useful doesn't mean you should put up with anything—you are entitled by law to basic employment rights. The National Association of Student Employment Services (NASES) website details your rights, and can help if you have difficulties with an employer.

Back to the sofa?

Of course the best place to begin your search is your careers advice centre—you can use your local university careers service in your home town, although priority may be given to students of the university. There are a bewildering number of options open to you during the summer so it's a good idea to call in and decide in advance what you're after. With a bit of foresight, you can set yourself up for a summer that's not only useful in the long run but good fun as well. Now where's that remote gone?

HOW TO MILK IT

How your casual job, broken down into tasks, could look on paper:
- ✔ **Kept yourself motivated whilst carrying out unskilled and repetitive tasks**
- ✔ **Dealt directly with the public—and hopefully stayed calm if they got abusive!**
- ✔ **Picked up office skills such as using a fax, answering the phone and using computers**
- ✔ **Obtained an insight into the commercial implications of your work**
- ✔ **Worked as part of a team**
- ✔ **Learned to communicate with people at different levels in an organisation.**

FAQS

I've got a long summer when I don't have to do anything other than sunbathe—why should I bother sorting out work experience?
Of course that is one option: go back to your parents', lie on the sofa watching endless hours of daytime telly and shout for 'room service' every time you feel a tad peckish. It is tempting, admittedly, but very quickly becomes boring. The thing is that your university holidays are the longest you will have in your life (barring sabbaticals, retirement and winning the lottery). The possibilities for doing something both fun and productive are

almost endless, so if you don't take such a unique opportunity now you will regret it later on. And that's just the nice answer—the nasty answer is that, as more and more employers demand a certain level of work experience from their graduate job applicants, you would severely damage your chances of getting your dream job if you spent the summer in a hammock.

I want to stay in my university city over the summer and get a job. Where to should I start looking?

A good place to start is your university careers service or job shop; they will often have several local employers looking for students, and may even have some in the specific career area you're thinking of. Specialist recruitment agencies will also take people on for summer schemes, although it's best to contact them as early as possible. And of course temping agencies can find you many types of work. To cover all bases, why not send speculative letters to some dream employers in your area asking for a work experience opportunity, as well as registering with an agency (remember that speculative letters should always be followed up with a phone call)? Either way, the end result should be career-prospect-boosting work experience. Your family would appreciate a visit at some point though!

I've already got a part-time job in an office and they've offered me a full-time position over the summer. But will this impress employers when I come to look for a graduate job?

Whether you're in your home town or hanging around your university, it's worth remembering that virtually any work you do can enhance your CV. You may think shovelling burgers or filing files for a filing company cannot be construed as 'worthwhile'—not so. From an employer's point of view, doing work over the summer demonstrates a good work ethic and is proof of experience of a working environment. Employers want to be reassured that you will be able to cope with the workplace and get on with your colleagues. The last thing they want is someone who'll pass out when confronted by an angry client or a missed deadline. This is where casual work comes in; according to many employers, graduates often show a frustrating lack of transferable skills such as good communication, teamwork, time management and initiative. Experiencing almost any workplace environment will help you to build on these.

WHERE NEXT?
goWales (for opportunities in Wales): **www.gowales.co.uk**
Graduate Advantage, West Midlands:
www.graduateadvantage.co.uk
Graduate Link, Yorkshire and Humberside: **www.graduatelink.com**
National Association of Student Employment Services (NASES):
www.nases.org.uk
Shell STEP (for placements with companies): **www.step.org.uk**

TAKING A GAP YEAR

THE BASICS

Need a break while you figure out your ideal career? Always wanted to travel the world? Accepted a job with deferred entry? Fed up with the stresses of academic life? Have a break . . . have a gap year!

Gap year, year out, year off—they're all names for the same thing. Whatever you call them, they're a big favourite with students and graduates these days. There's also a growing number of career gappers—people who take a career break to go travelling. So even if you want to get started on your career now, you still have a chance for a gap year later on.

150,000 young people take a gap year, either between A levels and university or immediately after graduating.

Why do a gap year?

A gap year, before or after university, has lots of advantages—you could travel the world or get some work experience before settling into a job. With so many students taking gap years these days, it's essential you do something worthwhile in your year out. Don't just use it as an excuse to watch daytime TV for a year—employers will spot a year casually 'missed out' of your CV. Remember while you're taking a gap year that you'll have to sell it to employers in the future—it can look pretty impressive on your CV. You might not realise it at the time, but living in the jungle, working for a year or making your way around Peru on your own is a big deal and shows you have a lot of skills and qualities that employers really want.

What should you do?

Gap years come in many forms, and you can choose just what you want to do with your year off. You can seize your last chance to travel the world before settling down to start a career. If you love *The Lord of the Rings*, explore New Zealand. Feeling generous? You could volunteer to help others by teaching at a primary school in Uganda, or working with a coral reef conservation project in Fiji (see the next chapter for a closer look at volunteering). A gap year doesn't have to be abroad: many people stay in this country and try out all kinds of things.

Of course, you can combine these options. Many people work for six months, saving up so they can spend the next six months travelling. Others prefer to travel first—and pay off their credit cards when they return. You can often find casual work when travelling (but make sure you have the right kind of visa) and fund your trip that way.

Take advantage of the opportunity to do something new, before you get tied down by a job, a house, a family . . . Whatever you choose to do, a gap year is a great opportunity to try new things—and may help you decide what to do with your life.

PLANNING YOUR ESCAPE

You can't just hop on the first plane out of Heathrow. Before you start your gap year, you need to do some serious planning.

What to do

First you have to decide what you want to do. Whether you want to travel the world, help people in need, or start working on your career, there are gap years to suit every taste and budget. You don't have to be a saint to volunteer on a project, nor are you selfish if you don't. Not all backpackers have bad clothes, huge hiking boots and filthy hair—it's a travel option for anyone. Doing an internship may start you on a career for life, but taking time off from your pursuit of a career will not hinder you. A gap year may be your last chance to do whatever your heart desires—so get out there and do it!

Where to go

If you've decided to travel, find out about the countries you're visiting. There are loads of guide books available—the Rough Guide and Lonely Planet series are particularly popular with gappers. These books are essential reading before you go and while you're there. They usually give you background info, maps of the country and its cities, and contain lists of places to visit and cheap accommodation. You can also find information on the web—there are dozens of websites devoted to gap years. Check the Foreign Office's list of countries that are not safe to visit, and avoid them.

What to wear

Think about climate—do you need to pack t-shirts, a raincoat or a woolly jumper? Make sure you take clothes that will be comfortable and hard-wearing. Consider the cultural and religious values. Will you be able to wear vest tops, or do you need to invest in some lightweight long-sleeved shirts? Bear in mind that you are a guest in the country, and try to avoid offending people. If you can't do without your hotpants, feel free to take them—but don't be surprised if you get some funny looks.

If you're planning to visit religious buildings and sacred sites, find out about their customs. Before entering a mosque, you should remove your shoes to show respect. Women may be asked to cover their heads in mosques and temples, so take a scarf or shawl. If you're wearing shorts or a short skirt, you may be refused entry to some cathedrals and churches.

What to say

Do you need to learn the language? Even if most locals know English, it's often useful to know a few basic phrases (hello, goodbye, thank you). And if they don't, make sure you know enough to get by. You could get a phrasebook and dig it out every time you want to speak, or you can learn the language at evening classes or from tapes. If you spend a long time in one place, you'll pick up the language naturally, but it can help to know some words before you start. Knowing a foreign language may be a great asset when you return home and look for a job.

FINDING THE FUNDS

The only bad thing about a gap year is the cost. Travelling is not exactly a cheap activity, but there are many ways to raise the money.

If you've been a very sensible student, you may have some money left over from those nice people at the Student Loans Company, which you can spend on your gap year. Then again, you might have had a life at university, in which case you're going to need to raise the funds yourself.

Set yourself a target. Figure out how much you need to earn each week, and stick to it. Volunteer projects will tell you how much to raise and you should be able to get some of this through fundraising. If you'll be travelling, set a budget for transport, accommodation, food, insurance, anything you need to buy before you go—and fun. Include some emergency money, as most travellers spend more than they expect. If you won't reach your target before your departure date, reassess—you may need to shorten your trip, skip the skydiving, or work while you're away.

If you find a job and become a semi-hermit, you'll quickly save up enough money for your plane ticket. If you continue to have a social life it'll take a bit longer, but you'll get there. An office job may develop skills useful in your future job-hunting. You may find a company willing to take you on for a few months, perhaps as maternity cover. Registering with a temp agency may help you to find short-term positions. Being the office dogsbody can be much more bearable if it only lasts a week in each place. Factory work is dull but easily obtainable, and if you work the off shifts you'll be raking it in. Bar work may be a little more exciting, but you'll be more tempted to spend. Work in a restaurant and you may get tips to supplement your pay.

Borrowing money is an option for those who can't wait to leave the rain behind. Credit cards can seem a great way to pay for your travel but watch out for high interest rates. You may end up paying twice what you spent if you get a card with bad rates. Your bank is unlikely to give you a loan to go travelling, as they have no guarantee of repayment, but if you have a job offer for your return you may be able to convince them that it's viable. Some parents are willing to lend funds enabling their offspring to travel. If you take advantage of this offer, set the terms for paying them back on your return.

If you're considering a gap year project, don't be put off by the expense. Fundraising for the trip may be daunting, but your gap year organisation should give you ideas and support. The organisational and marketing skills you develop will look great on your CV. Bear that in mind when you're struggling to convince friends and relatives to pay for you to spend six months in Fiji. Reminding them that it's for a good cause may loosen their purse strings. Many volunteers offer their sponsors a presentation about their project on their return. This is a great way of thanking them, and gives you a chance to practise public speaking. If you're really persuasive, you might find a company to sponsor your trip and give you a job on your return.

Raising the money for your trip may take some time, but don't get frustrated. Remember that the hours of boredom will bring days of pleasure when you're away.

A GAP YEAR IN THE UK

Deferred your entry for a grad scheme? Still not sure what career path to choose? Taking time out for work experience in the UK could be the answer.

Work it out

A year's work is great to put on your CV when you finally come round to starting a career—plus it will pay off some of those debts. Recruitment agencies will help you to find short-term jobs, which are a great way to get some office experience. If you're more interested in money than job satisfaction, warehouse or factory work is often available and unpopular shifts tend to pay quite well. Bar and restaurant work is also popular. A long period of work experience, whatever it is, may help to impress recruiters later.

Give it a try

Work experience is the best thing since sliced bread for many employers, so having a year or just a few months on your CV will look pretty impressive. Doing work experience or an internship is an opportunity to try out various jobs without long-term commitment and find out what might be right for you. You could spend a week shadowing a family friend, or do a six-month placement with a major organisation. Some employers pay a normal wage; others pay nothing, but you may receive travel or lunch money.

Have an adventure

Remember going on school trips when you were a kid? Now it's your turn to be the sadistic instructor! There are children's activity centres all over Britain, specialising in adventure weeks for school groups and holidays for children. These trips promote teamwork, cooperation and the development of social skills. If you're an active sort you could teach water sports or mountain climbing. Staff are also required behind the scenes—preparing food, cleaning and in administration.

Charity begins at home . . .

You don't have to travel halfway round the planet to do voluntary work: there are plenty of projects seeking volunteers in this country. If you've been involved in a local charity, you could see if they need help. Chances are they would be unable to pay you, but you would gain invaluable experience—and you could earn money working in a bar in the evenings. You could find a volunteer placement in a different region. Community Service Volunteers (CSV) organises community-based placements all over the UK, supporting people in need and enabling them to develop their lives. CSV provides accommodation and meals, plus a small weekly allowance.

SELLING YOUR EXPERIENCE

You've just returned, jetlagged and tanned from six months in Australia. You're ready to apply for jobs—but what's the best way to make your year out experiences attractive to prospective employers?

Research has shown that future employers are impressed by candidates who have done something useful in their gap year. It's up to you to persuade them that you've done just that. If you've done voluntary work, or paid work, you've obviously done something useful and will have plenty of skills to show for it. Even a year spent backpacking will have helped you to develop those essential 'soft skills'; you just need to know how to present them. Prospective employers will not, however, be impressed by your expert knowledge of *Hollyoaks* and *Deal Or No Deal*.

Great skills

Many employers feel that universities don't sufficiently develop the 'soft skills' necessary in the world of work. These skills are often picked up during a year out. If you've spent six months teaching English, you'll have fabulous communication skills, and may be a good leader. Involvement in the construction of a well in Somalia will have tested your teamwork abilities, and you may have shown leadership qualities. Just choosing to leave the security of home demonstrates that you're eager for a challenge and willing to face new situations. Travelling independently requires organisational ability and increases independence and confidence. Working to save up for the trip shows you are highly motivated. You may have picked up other skills, such as foreign languages, along the way. Although it may seem a little backward, taking time off before starting your career may actually help you to achieve that all-important promotion sooner.

Broad mind

Employers look for interesting people, who would do the job well and be a pleasure to work with. They'll see loads of applications from graduates with great qualifications. You need a way to stand out from the crowd— and your gap year could just do it. Travelling is renowned for broadening the mind, and you're sure to have stretched your horizons along the way.

Seeing new places and meeting new people will have taught you about other cultures and lifestyles. You're likely to have a far more mature attitude, compared with applicants coming straight from university.

Firm commitment

A few employers may be worried about your commitment levels. If you've become accustomed to a mobile lifestyle, moving on whenever you get bored, what's to keep you from wandering off when you've had a tough week at work? You may have to convince them that you're back for good. Perhaps your wanderlust is sated after a globetrotting year, or the 'delights' of Thai toilets awakened you to the comforts of life in a developed country. You may crave stability, so you can put down roots and develop more than transitory friendships.

WHERE NEXT?

BUNAC: **www.bunac.org.uk**

Community Service Volunteers (CSV): **www.csv.org.uk**

doctorjob.com: **doctorjob.com/gapyear**

Foreign and Commonwealth Office (click on the 'Travel Advice' tab): **www.fco.gov.uk**

GoGapYear.com: **www.gogapyear.com**

International projects: **www.i-to-i.com**

Lonely Planet: **www.lonelyplanet.com**

Lonely Planet Thorn Tree forum: **thorntree.lonelyplanet.com**

Volunteering in England: **www.volunteering.org.uk**

Voluntary Work Overseas: **www.vso.org.uk**

UNDERTAKING VOLUNTARY WORK

VOLUNTEERING IS THE NEW BACKPACKING . . .

Rather than join the stampede of students drinking their way across Australia, why not get a bit more from your time overseas?

This year, thousands of wide-eyed students and graduates will travel the globe to try their hand at anything from turtle-tagging to social work, from farm labouring to community teaching. As well as helping eco-systems and local communities in some of the most beautiful places in the world, many will arrive back in the UK armed with new skills that can be transferred immediately to the workplace. Being able to demonstrate the commitment and versatility required for often demanding projects is a major plus point in the opinion of prospective employers.

For many, volunteering is more about opening up their lives to different experiences and doing something constructive with their time. The career skills they pick up are often an unexpected but welcome by-product.

Either way, the truth of the matter is that voluntary work will do wonders for your CV. In today's ultra-competitive job market, employers look for people who demonstrate personal development as well as traditional office-based skills. Gaining insights into other cultures and adapting quickly to a different environment are part of the job of being a volunteer, and are the kind of qualities that prospective employers can't get enough of. Many say that adapting to a different way of life was one of the most valuable things they took away from the experience. And getting rid of inhibitions and being more confident were also bonuses.

Wish you were here?

It may be the new backpacking, but that doesn't mean voluntary work is a holiday. Volunteers have to forget any thoughts that a placement might involve lying around, sipping a beer and idly counting the odd turtle.

Planning ahead

So the benefits are clear, but what's the best way to organise voluntary work? You may feel happier going though a reputable organisation which arranges the transport, logistics and paperwork for you, as well as providing support if something goes wrong. The downside of this is that it can cost upwards of £1,250 just to get on to the volunteer placement. This will cover basic food and accommodation, but often not transport and travel.

It is possible to do research and arrange a volunteer placement off your own back. There are thousands of conservation schemes around, which rely heavily on volunteers. But you must be prepared for it to be more disorganised—always have a back-up plan if it all falls through. Because, whether it's saving the turtles in Costa Rica, running a community radio station in Ghana or working with street children in India, the experience of working hard and being somewhere completely new will go a long way to help you along whatever career path you choose.

DOS AND DON'TS OF VOLUNTEERING OVERSEAS

DO have a real think about what kind of work you want to do. There are endless opportunities out there to suit your chosen career path or the personal skills you want to develop.

DO spend time researching the local culture and traditions of the country you're travelling to and make an effort to learn the local language. You'll get a lot more out of the experience and find it easier to meet people.

DO put time aside to travel afterwards. Volunteering, particularly for conservation projects, can mean that you're staying in remote areas with limited transport and contact with the outside world.

If you're going through an agency **DO** ask for contact details of people who have already done a placement. It's useful to talk to them about the reality and day-to-day routine of the work.

DO look at your insurance details very carefully. Check whether you need your own cover and whether the organisation's insurance includes medical cover for the work you may be doing, and travel back to the UK in an emergency.

DON'T think that volunteering is an extended holiday in the sun. On volunteer projects you will be expected to pull your weight and work hard in sometimes difficult and uncomfortable conditions.

DON'T expect the same luxuries you get at home. Volunteer projects in poor countries often mean a very plain diet, basic accommodation and limited hot water and electricity.

WHERE NEXT?

Africa and Asia Venture (three-month teaching placements at primary or secondary schools [with a month's travel afterwards] throughout Africa, India or Nepal): **www.aventure.co.uk**
African Conservation Experience (arrange for people to work on placements in game and nature reserves throughout southern Africa): **www.conservationafrica.net**
Biosphere Expeditions (offers hands-on, non-profit conservation expeditions for nothing): **www.biosphere-expeditions.org**
BTCV International Conservation Holidays (organises working holidays on conservation and environmental projects in Europe, North America, Asia, Africa and Australia): **www.btcv.org**

Challenges Worldwide (an educational charity which offers placements for volunteers in Antigua, Bangladesh, Belize, Dominica, Ecuador and Tasmania): **www.challengesworldwide.com**
doctorjob.com for advice on voluntary and charity work: **doctorjob.com/charity**
Earthwatch Institute (placements on environmental, conservation, archaeology and scientific research overseas): **www.earthwatch.org**
Gap Activity Projects (GAP; aimed at school-leavers wanting a year out before higher education, training or work. GAP has projects in over 30 countries): **www.gap.org.uk**
ICA:UK (one-year placements with local development organisations worldwide): **www.ica-uk.org.uk**
Inter-Cultural Youth Exchange (ICYE-UK; placements include drug rehabilitation programmes, working with street children, human rights projects and HIV programmes): **www.icye.co.uk**
International Directory of Voluntary Work (a thorough guide to short-term and long-term voluntary work overseas): **www.vacationwork.co.uk**
i-to-i (provides TEFL training and volunteer projects worldwide): **www.i-to-i.com**
Raleigh International (provides young people [17 to 25] with the opportunity to work on community and environmental projects for three months): **www.raleigh.org.uk**
TimeBank (the national campaign to raise the profile of voluntary work): **www.timebank.org.uk**
VSO (Voluntary Services Overseas; offers volunteers a chance to share skills and experience with people in around 60 developing countries): **vso.org.uk**

WEIGHING UP THE PROS AND CONS OF DOING A FURTHER DEGREE

WHY CONTINUE TO POSTGRADUATE LEVEL?

If your degree didn't satisfy your hunger for knowledge, and all those pot noodles and late-night essays haven't put you off, you might be considering postgraduate study.

Having a love of a subject can produce the most dedicated students, but it is definitely worth thinking about whether or not your chosen course really fits in with your long-term career plans. With the ever-expanding number of new undergraduate degree courses and universities, a postgraduate qualification certainly distinguishes you from the crowd, particularly in today's competitive job market.

But for every postgraduate that walks straight into their dream job and starts earning megabucks, there's another left with a meaningless certificate and a meaningful overdraft. Postgraduate study is a major investment of both time and money, so it's essential to research what the benefits are to you. In some sectors postgraduate qualifications are essential, in others they will improve your employment prospects and in others recruiters will be more interested in your transferable skills and work experience. So find out how your potential employers view applicants with postgraduate qualifications and whether it really makes a difference.

Motivation is key

It's important to consider your reasons and motivation for continuing to postgraduate level before starting on a period of intensive study and financial pressures. There's nothing worse than finding yourself half way through a course that's crippling your finances and realising you don't want to finish it—it's an expensive mistake to make, and not the best thing to have to explain to employers at interview!

It's also important to realise that a postgraduate qualification doesn't guarantee you a job, particularly if you choose a course which isn't directly related to your chosen career. When it comes to getting a job you'll have to justify your decision to potential employers, and you'll be up against people who have spent their time gaining valuable work experience while you've been studying.

So, it's decision time. Which reason best describes your decision to undertake postgraduate study?

1   To improve my career prospects
2   To fulfil my intellectual ambition and provide me with a personal challenge
3   To give myself more time for making those dreaded decisions about my career

Good reasons to keep on studying

Converting to a new field can be a good reason for following the postgraduate route after graduation. Masters or diploma courses often offer the best way into an area of work that your undergraduate degree alone excludes you from. You may have chosen a career path that clearly requires further study, such as teaching or law, in which case there are specific courses available. Even if you don't stay with these professions for life, you will gain valuable transferable skills from such courses.

It is also possible to 'convert' to a new sector whilst working. Many employers welcome applications from graduates of all disciplines and provide professional training and support for them in their chosen area, such as accountancy.

In some fields, especially when competition is fierce, a postgraduate qualification can make all the difference. For example, a few of the leading investment banks now target postgraduates specifically for their advanced analytical skills. For MBAs, some employers have special programmes but they do generally require three to five years' work experience, so it's always best to check with your favoured employer first before embarking on a course.

The wrong reasons for staying in education

Be honest with yourself—postgraduate study is expensive and much more taxing than an undergraduate degree, and you'll regret it if you put yourself under financial and emotional pressure because you couldn't think of anything better to do. You have to want to do your course, for whatever reason, or you won't complete it.

If you're unsure of what you want to do and think that postgraduate study is the perfect way to buy a bit more time, as well as prolonging your student days, then it's probably best to think again. Not only will this lack of focus mean that you may choose a course that might not help you on your eventual career path, but it is also unlikely that a further year of study will, in itself, help to make up your mind.

Another tempting route onto a postgraduate course is simply an offer of a place by your tutors, not least because partial or total funding is usually attached. But this isn't necessarily a good reason to take it up. Again, you need to be sure that it's something you actually want to do and that your current institution is the right place to do it. Staying where you are may appear to be an easy option, but it could easily backfire if you agree to such an offer without researching all of the options open to you.

Undeniably, the worst reason to embark on postgraduate study is to compensate for a disappointing degree result. 'It's common to presume that employers will be blinded by a masters, but that really isn't the case,' agrees Laura. 'If you are disappointed with your degree result you need to think about why you got that grade—are you likely to be a better postgraduate student? If not, you may benefit more from getting relevant work experience to impress employers.'

DON'T DO A POSTGRADUATE DEGREE IF . . .

✔ you can't think of anything else to do
✔ your boyfriend/girlfriend is still studying and you'll miss him/her if you leave
✔ you're biding time because you can't face those tough career decisions
✔ you want to put 'Dr' in front of your name
✔ you just can't get a job
✔ you want to gain an extended visit to another country
✔ you want to stay on at your university and re-live old times
✔ you want to be an eternal student and can't bear the thought of joining the 'real world'

WHAT COURSES ARE AVAILABLE?

UK postgraduate courses are either research-based, by instruction (taught courses) or a mixture of both. You'll need to read up on your desired course's contents and structure and decide which is best for you.

Here's an idea of what some of the most popular courses involve.

RESEARCH-BASED COURSES

Doctorates (PhD/DPhil)
✔ three to four years full time
✔ five to six years part time
✔ considered very intellectually challenging
✔ includes a thesis of around 100,000 words and usually an oral presentation
✔ entry requirement: 2:1 or higher/relevant Master's

Masters (MPhil)
✔ two to three years full time

✔ four to five years part time

✔ similar in structure to a Doctorate, only shorter

✔ many of those who register for an MPhil transfer to a PhD

✔ includes a thesis of around 60,000 words and usually an oral presentation

✔ entry requirement: 2:1 or higher

TAUGHT COURSES

✔ Masters (MA, MSc, MBA)

✔ one to two years full time

✔ two to three years part time

✔ includes seminars, lectures, tutorials, project work, oral work, some research, a thesis/dissertation and exams. The balance between these varies.

✔ entry requirement: 2:2 or higher/postgraduate diploma

Postgraduate diplomas and certificates

✔ one year full time

✔ two years part time

✔ vocational or practical conversion courses

✔ includes continuous assessment/extended essay/coursework/exams

✔ entry requirement: open to graduates of any discipline, check with individual institutions concerning the required grade

Postgraduate certificate in education (PGCE)

✔ one year full time

✔ This is the widely accepted qualification to achieve teacher status. It includes preparation for class lessons, setting homework and exams and teaching practice in local schools.

✔ entry requirement: open to graduates of any discipline. Check with individual institutions concerning the required grade.

✔ centralised admissions and clearing system through the

Graduate Teacher Training Registry. See Where next? for contact information.

WHERE TO STUDY

Choosing where to study will require more thought than shutting your eyes and sticking a pin in a map.

Committing yourself to spending the next year or two in a place you hate can be as disheartening as choosing the wrong course, and in some cases can make you unhappy enough to give it all up.

Things you should consider

Studying your postgrad degree in Jamaica or the Seychelles may not be an option, but if you consider the following you should end up somewhere that you enjoy living, despite the rain:

✔ Staying on at your undergraduate institution has its advantages: a familiar environment, culture and surroundings will help you to settle into your new degree easily, and you know about facilities and staff.

✔ On the other hand, you may be ready for a change. Find out about the reputation of the university, not only for postgraduate study in general but also for your course specifically.

✔ How does the content of the course you want to study differ from one university to another?

✔ Do you feel comfortable in a city environment, or would you rather live somewhere quieter?

✔ Do you prefer a campus environment?

✔ Accommodation and living costs are cheaper in some parts of the UK than others. If money is an important factor, it's important to consider this.

✔ If you have to live off-campus, can you get to and from your lectures easily?

✔ Does the university provide accommodation for postgrads?
✔ Does the university have a thriving postgraduate community?

WHEN TO STUDY

Once you've decided you're ready for postgraduate study, you need to think about when to start your course.

Most people will start straight after their undergraduate degree, but there are other options. Some people take a gap year or time out first, some get a couple of years' 'real life' and work experience under their belts, and some manage to study and work at the same time. Here are some of the pros and cons of each choice:

Going postgrad straight after completing your degree

This is the most common, and for many the most convenient, choice. You haven't got any other ties or responsibilities such as a job, so it's an easy time to continue studying. However, some courses will require you to have relevant work experience, which you'll have to gain before returning to your studies. You should also consider things like lack of funds, boredom and demotivation after three or four years of study. Do you really want to go straight back to university without a break?

Returning to study after a gap year or time out

You may want to take some time out after graduating and before returning to university for a postgrad course. However, you will need to think about making arrangements concerning when to apply, admission exams and interviews. These things become more difficult to deal with if you're in another country, and you may find you don't have the inclination to do so. If you leave it too late, though, you'll find yourself back home in no time with nowhere to study and all application deadlines passed.

Leaving work to study

Would you give up a full-time, permanent job to continue with your education? Once you've gained some experience and relevant skills and are earning money, it can become tempting not to make the break but to stay at work. There are ways around cutting yourself off from your valued job, though. You could ask your employer for a leave of absence such as a sabbatical, where they hold your position open for you while you study for a postgraduate degree. Issues to consider include returning to academic study, the shock of no longer earning and re-entry to work after your postgrad degree. You should also consider whether it would be more beneficial to stay on at work and continue gaining experience, or to study and then return to work with an additional qualification.

Combining work and study

If you don't want to give up work while you study, you could try part-time study or distance learning. Some jobs, such as accountancy, will require you to study for qualifications while working, but it's also possible to combine work with postgrad study in an unrelated subject. A note of caution—do not underestimate how tiring juggling work and study can be. Make sure you work out before you undertake your postgrad degree how many hours you will need to study per week, and only take on what is possible. Don't go for this option unless you are very disciplined.

COMPETING FOR JOBS

This well-meaning advice is definitely not directed at those postgrads who are going on to do post-docs, lectureships, yet more study or industry jobs related to their discipline. These are the lucky ones in some ways—if often the underpaid ones. No, this section is aimed at those who had a very nice time as a postgrad, thank you, but have decided to go back into the mainstream of graduate recruitment.

The good news

In some ways, this is a classic careers non-issue. Consider the case of law students whose long vigils in the library with only pro-plus for company have put them off law for life. Think about the engineers who realise in their final year that engineering is an undervalued, underpaid area of work.

These people think they've got a career crisis on their hands, but soon make the startling discovery that over 40 percent of graduate jobs are open to graduates from any discipline. All of these jobs are open to post graduates from any discipline too. In fact, if you've done a numerate subject there'll be another 10 to 20 percent of graduate jobs open to you on top of that. Add to that your added maturity and newly-developed postgrad skills (presentation, writing, editing, self-reliance, use of IT, team-work in some cases, teaching skills in others—adapt the list to fit your own experiences) and you should have the edge over the undergrad riff-raff.

The bad news

Employers won't understand or even care about the labour of love that was your thesis topic. They may not even have heard of your qualification—did *you* know what a DipHE or MSt was before you got one? And they certainly won't want to read even the most eloquent chapter of your dissertation. Your new challenge is to translate the skills that you've acquired during your postgrad years into words that they not only understand but value. These are probably the kind of words that they use in their own adverts and brochures: things like 'communication', 'analysis', 'adaptability' and others.

If you're under 30, it's likely that your age won't be an issue, but you should expect to tackle some difficult questions about why you didn't embark on this career straight out of university and how committed you are to it now. That's just the interview game, though, and you shouldn't take apparently aggressive questions too personally. Just use your superior intellect to develop killer answers to the killer questions.

You could be up against people who have spent their time since graduating working in industry. So you will need to be able to justify your decision to choose postgraduate study when it comes to applying for jobs. But for the right sector and the right employer, your postgraduate qualification can really tip the balance in your favour.

Finally, the worst news. They won't pay you any more than their first-degree-only recruits, unless your further study is in some way relevant to the job and gives you the edge in some way. But, hey, it's nearly always better paid than staying in academia, so who's counting?

SEVEN GOLDEN RULES OF POSTGRADUATE STUDY

1   **Do it for the right reasons.** A postgraduate course is a major investment of time and money, so you need to be clear about why you're doing it and what you're going to get out of it. Have a look at the good and bad reasons listed above, and work out which side you fall.

2   **Pick the right type of course and study option.** You can study pretty much anything at postgraduate level, and in any way, be it part time, full time or 'flexible' learning, which could be a mixture of online lectures and real-life tutorials. If you have a burning desire to investigate a topic in more detail, you could do a standard taught course or a research degree. And then you could study for a postgraduate diploma (often a vocational course to train you for a specific career), a doctorate (or PhD, which includes independent research and, often, teaching) or a masters of arts/science (or MA/MSc, for those who want to develop their academic understanding of a subject). You could also do a masters of business administration (MBA), which focuses entirely on business-related issues. Employers normally recruit MBA students at a higher level than first-degree students, and to get on an MBA course you'll need to have several years' work experience under your belt.

3   **Find the institution that's right for you.** You'll need to consider lots of things, such as entry requirements (good courses will have interviews and minimum entry requirements), the rating, location and reputation of the institution and any employer links. You should investigate whether there are opportunities to complete industry placements and talk to former students about what they thought of the course, and also if it helped them get work.

4   **Get funding if you can.** Postgraduate study is an expensive

business—the main expenses are fees and the cost of living. There is help available for course fees, but competition can be tough; so try to investigate funding sources early in the final year of your first degree. You could combine a number of funding sources, such as public funding bodies, institutional funding or career development loans. You could arrange bursaries (for some vocational courses such as social work or teaching in shortage subjects) or sponsorship from large companies. You may also want to get in touch with educational charities and trusts. Whatever you do, do it as early as you can.

5 **Investigate studying overseas.** Studying abroad can be an attractive option—employers will be impressed with your initiative and resourcefulness, and you may have the opportunity to improve your language skills. But it can also be a tricky affair—competition is fierce and places and funding can often take much longer to organise. Before you do anything, make sure the courses are acceptable to professional bodies and employers in the UK. There may also be language requirements or pre-entry exams, such as the GRE (Graduate Record Examinations) or GMAT (Graduate Management Admission Test) in the US. The Fulbright Commission facilitates study in the US for British students. For study in Europe, have a look at the *FEDORA Guide to Postgraduate Study in Europe*—your careers service should have a reference copy.

6 **Know when to apply.** The general rule is that you should do your research in your penultimate year, and then apply for places in January of your final year. Certain courses have their own closing dates. For example, applications for the primary-level PGCE should be in by mid-December. Applications for law courses also have set dates.

7 **Get some help.** Before you do anything, try to talk to careers advisers, course tutors, employers and former postgrad students. Look out for postgrad events run by your careers

service. You can also get tips and advice from the links below, or from your university careers service website.

WHERE NEXT?

doctorjob (for courses, institution profiles and advice on funding): **doctorjob.com/postgrad**
Association of MBAs: **www.mbaworld.com**
British Council (information on awards for overseas students studying in the UK): **www.britishcouncil.org.uk**
Career Development Loans: **www.lifelonglearning.co.uk/cdl**
Department for Education and Skills Higher Education (general info, including on financial support):
www.dfes.gov.uk/highereducation
Department for Work and Pensions (advice on benefits available to full- and part-time students): **www.dwp.gov.uk**
The Fulbright Commission (facilitates study in the US for British students): **www.fulbright.co.uk**
Graduate Teacher Training Registry (GTTR; 0870 1122205):
www.gttr.ac.uk
Higher Education Funding Council for England (HEFCE; details of higher education funding for institutions): **www.hefce.ac.uk**

Main funding bodies in the UK
Arts and Humanities Research Board (AHRB): **www.ahrb.ac.uk**
Biotechnology and Biological Sciences Research Council (BBSRC):
www.bbsrc.ac.uk
Economic and Social Research Council (ESRC): **www.esrc.ac.uk**
Medical Research Council (MRC): **www.mrc.ac.uk**
Natural Environment Research Council (NERC): **www.nerc.ac.uk**
Particle Physics and Astronomy Research Council (PPARC):
www.pparc.ac.uk
postgradireland (for course information in Ireland):
postgradireland.com

PRIVATE SECTOR OR PUBLIC SECTOR?

GOING PUBLIC

If you want your work to do more than affect the profit margins of an already successful company, the public sector could be the place for you.

It's an uber-sector that encompasses a mélange of different jobs relating to the efficient running of the country through the emergency services, government, Civil Service, local councils, the armed forces and health services. You can do many of the jobs you'd traditionally associate with the private sector and you'll be treated nicely, invited to work hours that suit you, and brought cups of tea while you do them. Okay, so that last part might be a bit of a fib, but while working in the public sector doesn't guarantee you a 'job for life' or a cushy slide into retirement it will provide a stimulating and diverse range of roles working for an organisation where your health and happiness is key.

The Civil Service has been criticised in the past for being over-staffed and inefficient. The government has pledged to tackle this—but that doesn't mean that there is a lack of graduate jobs available. In fact, central government recruiters are keen to get their hands on talented new graduates in order to help to create a more effective and efficient service. This emphasis on improving services means that employees are also actively encouraged to experience work in the private sector, where saving money and working efficiently are traditionally important. The largest increases in public sector employment in recent years have been in health and social work and education, and there are shortage areas in local government that need

61

more graduates. Engineering, environmental health, trading standards, social work and social care, planning, library work, legal work, teaching, educational psychology and occupational therapy are all areas which require more applicants. With all these changes afoot, public service work is anything but dull.

IN THE MIX

Everyone likes to have some variety in their job. A bit of this, a bit of that, maybe a trip to the stationery cupboard if you're feeling crazy.

One of the best things about working in the public sector is the range of opportunities to work in almost any area and the variety of tasks available once you're in. You never know with these public sector types what they might have in store for you. One minute you're doing some photocopying, the next they've got you writing speeches for the PM. Wherever you work in the public sector, you will be given the opportunity to work on real projects that will make a significant difference to the way public services in the UK actually work and, unlike many positions in the private sector, you will be given a large amount of responsibility, including people-management roles, at an early stage.

2,000,000 people are employed by local government; it is one of the largest employers in the UK.

FEELING PERKY

With great benefits, rising salaries and the 'feel good' factor associated with giving something back to society, it's no wonder that graduates have woken up to what's on offer.

The lure of the public sector is undeniable. Year after year graduates are drawn to the generous benefits package and competitive salary. But applicants are wrong to assume that perks are all the public sector has to offer. Working for a public sector employer means that you can improve people's lives in a direct way, whether by researching and implementing policy at a strategic level or in the front-line, tackling people's everyday concerns.

Most of the perks associated with the public sector apply across the board, whether you're a civil servant or a fireman. You can expect fair salary scales with annual increases, flexible working arrangements, generous holiday entitlement, possible secondment opportunities to other departments, crèche facilities for parents with young children, good pension arrangements and the opportunity to work with all kinds of people.

Making a difference to the community

Working for a public sector employer means that you have the opportunity to affect more than a company's profit margin and can actually influence the way services are run for the community. The desire to make a positive impact on people's lives is often called the 'public sector ethos' and accounts for higher levels of job satisfaction in employees.

Equal opportunities

Equality and diversity issues are now top of the agenda for most employers, and none more so than those in the public sector. Public sector employers are particularly keen to recruit a diverse workforce so that they can effectively represent the community they serve, and, because of this, diversity is another area where public sector employers have taken the lead over their private sector counterparts.

The majority of public sector employees are women, and they hold 40 percent of managerial roles, 12 percent more than in the private sector. However, although ethnic minorities are well represented in the public sector as a whole, there are few in senior positions. The good news is that this figure is improving and there are targets to bring more members of ethnic minority groups into higher-level positions. Elsewhere, local councils have focused their attention on issues such as the underrepresentation of men in traditionally female careers (such as primary school teaching) and are attracting more applications from disabled people.

Finally, age legislation, which came into effect in 2006, makes it illegal for employers to refuse someone a job, promotion, training or benefits on the basis of their age, which is great news for mature and 'inexperienced' younger graduates alike.

So there you have it—everyone's invited to the public sector party!

Graduate-friendly

The organised little groups responsible for running the country have their own special systems in place to enable you to join them. There are lots of development schemes and training programmes, two of which are the Civil Service Fast Stream and the National Graduate Development Programme (NGDP). The NGDP enables graduates to have a broad experience of local government and leads to opportunities to become a specialist or remain a generalist, as well as providing a better understanding of the sector. The Civil Service Fast Stream offers an excellent training and development programme, which is also very saleable on your CV. There is excellent scope for development as the Civil Service invests a lot of time and money training its leaders of the future.

The benefits

Salaries are increasing to compare more favourably with those offered in the private sector. The benefits packages offered by public sector employers usually include a generous holiday entitlement of 25 days, a favourable pension scheme and flexible working options. Graduates who join the Fast Stream recruitment programme are assured a competitive salary and other benefits. There are also many other routes that can offer equally rewarding careers but perhaps begin on lower pay grades.

57% **The public sector has the highest retention rate of graduates recruited five years ago.** Source: Association of Graduate Recruiters

One thing that marks out a public sector employer is the emphasis placed on training and development. Central government employers are no different and will offer a wide range of personal and professional development opportunities, recognising that motivated and supported staff are usually more productive.

THE TRUTH ABOUT PUBLIC SECTOR SALARIES

If it intends to attract and retain good candidates, especially graduates, the public sector has to compete on salary. In the past few years, both pay and social esteem have been advancing in the public sector. Having played catch-up for a while, graduate starting salaries are finally competitive. According to the Association of Graduate Recruiters (AGR) the median graduate starting salary offered in 2006 by employers in the public sector was £19,900, which is only just below the median for all types of employer at £20,300.

PUBLIC vs PRIVATE

Few positions in the private sector can offer the same opportunities for growth and development as the majority of public sector roles.

Apart from the investment in training and development, there is more opportunity for secondment and cross-functional careers. Training and development can take many forms, from informal work shadowing and on-the-job training, to gaining qualifications such as NVQs, apprenticeships, postgraduate degrees or professional qualifications. Also, public sector workers get a great deal in terms of the all-important work–life balance.

15% of public sector workers usually work over 45 hours per week, compared with 23% in the private **sector.** Source: National Statistics Public Sector Employment Trends 2005 survey

For more on the civil service and central government, have a look at the industry profiles towards the end of this book.

WHERE NEXT?

You can find more information at: **doctorjob.com/publicservice**

The British Army: **www.army.mod.uk**

Civil Service Fast Stream: **www.faststream.gov.uk**

Civil Service Recruitment Gateway: **www.careers.civil-service.gov.uk**

Foreign & Commonwealth Office: **www.fco.gov.uk**

Government Communications Headquarters (GCHQ): **www.gchq.gov.uk**

Government Operational Research Service: **www.operational-research.gov.uk**

HM Revenue & Customs: **www.hmrc.gov.uk**

Local Government careers: **www.lgcareers.com**

Ministry of Defence and the armed forces: **www.mod.uk**

National graduate development programme (for careers in local government): **www.ngdp.co.uk**

NHS careers: **www.nhscareers.nhs.uk**

UK Police Service: **www.police.uk**

Royal Air Force careers: **www.rafcareers.com**

The Security Service: **www.mi5.gov.uk**

Working for an MP: **www.w4mp.org**

10

STARTING YOUR OWN BUSINESS

FINDING OUT MORE

More and more graduates are considering self-employment—and why not? If you have ambition and a decent idea, it's probably worth a go soon after you graduate. You won't have a lot to lose, you're used to working antisocial hours and, for many, it beats working for someone else.

Starting a business is particularly difficult for younger people because of various legal requirements and other constraints. It's hard to know just how successful the businesses run by young people are, as they tend to operate invisibly, either within a 'training for business' scheme or in a form of partnership with a relative. There are, however, many successful young entrepreneurs.

Take advice first. There is a lot of free advice offered to those wanting to start small businesses, so take advantage of every scrap. Banks have helpful information packs available and, generally speaking, helpful staff working in this area. Your local training and enterprise council (TEC) or local enterprise council (LEC) in Scotland licenses advisers to help you with your plans and stocks plenty of written information as well.

The essential elements are: thinking about the customers who will want and afford your goods or services; obtaining the financial backing; supplying the goods or services on time; and all the other logistical headaches involved in running your own business.

Why might I want to set up a business at this age?

There are many reasons why you might want to do down this route. You may have a strong interest or skill in a certain business area; you may want more independence and greater job satisfaction; the idea that any profits made will belong to you may also be a great incentive; you may look forward to feeling a sense of achievement and pride in the venture. If you're really serious about starting a business, you'll probably be a positive person, enthusiastic, and motivated to work hard and succeed. Also, you'll probably have fewer domestic commitments, like family or a mortgage, than many older people.

Potential pitfalls

Bear in mind that greater independence brings greater responsibility. Any business decisions will be down to you, and you'll also have to cope with any failures or problems faced by the business.

Lack of experience can cause serious problems in establishing credibility with both finance providers (for example, bank managers) and potential customers. Lack of qualifications, technical skills and business training can also hinder anyone starting a business. Banks especially may feel that a younger person can't possibly know enough about managing a business. You may well have work experience, but this is unlikely to be enough to convince potential backers or customers that you know what you're doing. You'll need to work much harder to prove yourself. A lack of confidence in your ability to run the business effectively can have an adverse effect on sales and profitability.

There are also legal issues to think about. If your planned business involves the use of certain industrial machinery, there may be age restrictions on its use; at the very least, full training will be required. A young person may be unable to hire or lease equipment. However, it may be possible to set up a hire/purchase agreement through a trusted friend or relative, who would act as a guarantor for payments to a given company. Alternatively a 'contract' could be established by which to pay them. While this could seem an uncomfortable situation, it may be the only way around the legal constraints.

Another potential problem is the lack of start-up finance. A few specialised loan funds exist to help people that most lenders won't assist because of their age, such as the 'Northern Youth Venture Fund', which is aimed at 18 to 30 year olds.

SCHEMES

Shell *Live*WIRE

Sponsored by Shell UK Ltd, Shell *Live*WIRE is the only national organisation providing free, extensive support and advice to 16 to 30 year olds from before start-up through to early growth. Every person making an enquiry receives an essential business kit which is tailored to their specific business idea. They are also put in touch with a local *Live*WIRE coordinator. The annual Young Business Start Up Awards give firms trading for less than 18 months the chance to compete for county, regional and national prizes, gaining publicity along the way.

The Prince's Trust

The Prince's Trust was established by the Prince of Wales in 1976 to help young people realise their full potential. Aimed at those aged 14–30 (or 14–25 in Scotland), the Trust offers support and financial assistance across a range of core programmes including business start-ups. Since 1983 the Trust has helped over 60,000 businesses, and its business programme currently offers a low-interest loan of up to £5,000, a marketing grant of up to £250, advice lines, seminars and access to a volunteer mentor.

GET PLANNING

Making good use of all advice will ensure that your planning is effective.

You can get support and advice from various organisations such as Job Centres, Learning and Skills Councils (LSCs) in England, Local Enterprise Councils (LECs) in Scotland, and the National Council for Education and Training in Wales, Business Links in England, Small Business Gateways in Scotland, Business Eyes in Wales, the Prince's Trust, the Prince's Scottish

Youth Business Trust and Chambers of Commerce. Trade associations may offer advice specific to a chosen business area.

Spend the time before you take the plunge in gaining relevant skills, experience, or finance. This could be through part-time paid employment or a placement. Where possible, your work placements should be with small businesses. You could negotiate with Job Centres to ensure that any training for work scheme offered to you is geared towards starting a business.

Gaining further qualifications may be essential to the success of some businesses. Having professional qualifications can gain credibility for your business. Any courses taken should be geared towards following a business career. Aim to combine specific subject knowledge with business skills, for example combining photography with business National Vocational Qualifications or marketing training. If there isn't a specific course available for the business idea, continue developing your skills as a hobby, while undertaking more conventional business training.

While getting practical work experience, draw up a comprehensive business plan, seek advice and research the market for your idea. Consider the costs of setting up, and think about premises, equipment and labour requirements. Develop as complete a picture as possible of the way your business should be running in the future.

The moral support and advice of parents, relatives and friends can be crucial in the early stages of business. You may need to rely on their financial assistance too, not only directly for the business, but also in terms of living expenses. Parental support can also be useful when establishing contacts and so on.

FOUR BUSINESS START-UP MISTAKES

1   **Not being fully committed.** Only people who are entirely committed to the idea should attempt to set up in business. It's a long hard slog for anyone, whatever their age, so don't think that exuberance and enthusiasm will get you through. They'll certainly help a lot, but there are other things to bear in mind and you'll almost certainly have to sacrifice some other areas of your life for a short time along the way.

2   **Not being fully prepared.** Plan your business approach as comprehensively as possible before you start up. A clear plan will be considered more positively by banks/sponsors/relatives and it will also be very useful to refer to when you start to manage your business once you're up and running. Make sure you're aware of legal and financial constraints that may affect you. You will need to think creatively to make your ideas become a reality.

3   **Not getting the right advice and support.** The nearest Business Link/Small Business Gateway/Business Eye or enterprise agency may be able to provide details of training schemes, loans and grants available in a particular area. The Prince's Trust may be able to help with grants towards training or equipment.

4   **Not thinking things through.** Do think long and hard about whether you want to start a business *now*. There are many advantages in getting some work experience before taking the plunge. That's not to say for a moment that you should abandon your plans completely, just that you should think about the timing very carefully.

WHERE NEXT?

Business Eye (Wales): **www.businesseye.org.uk**
Business Gateway (Scotland): **www.bgateway.com**
Business Link (England): **www.businesslink.gov.uk**
The Entrepreneur Test: **www.liraz.com/webquiz.htm**
Invest Northern Ireland: **www.investni.com**
Prince's Scottish Youth Business Trust: **www.psybt.org.uk**
Prince's Trust: **www.princes-trust.org.uk**
Shell *Live*WIRE: **www.shell-livewire.org**
Startups.co.uk: **www.startups.co.uk**
Young Enterprise UK: **www.young-enterprise.org.uk**
Young Entrepreneur: **www.youngentrepreneur.com**

GET
THAT JOB!

'SPINNING' YOUR CV

GETTING STARTED

Now that you've spent some time thinking about what you really want to do, and the fantastic skills you've got to help you to get there, you can focus on transferring all that essential information onto your CV.

Some people think that a fantastic CV alone will get them their dream job, but that's rarely the case. For most recruiters, checking through CVs forms a preliminary 'sifting' process, whereby they can look out for the people with the right skills, experience and suitability for a given role, and then fix a time to meet them in person.

The employment market has never been more competitive, and a personnel officer or recruiter can receive hundreds of CVs for every job opening. Even if you're registering with a job agency, you need to make sure that your CV looks impressive and well planned. Remember that you've only got a few seconds to capture someone's attention—you don't want it to be for the wrong reasons!

If your CV doesn't include any prior work experience, you should make sure you demonstrate the variety of transferable skills employers are looking for.

BEGIN AT THE END

Your CV is your chance to advertise your most marketable skills. Preparing a list of these may seem like hard work, but it is well worth doing.

This list will help you to write a more powerful CV, as well as to present yourself more professionally to a potential employer. It's also excellent preparation for an interview—you will feel confident about what you have to offer and will sell yourself better.

Involvement in university societies looks great on your CV.

Thinking about your career objective

Before writing your CV, you should have a very clear idea about which job you are looking for and the kind of company you would like to work for.

You might want to include your career objective at the top of your CV, directly after your contact details. This will help people know exactly what type of job you're looking for.

Be as specific as you can. It's not enough to say, 'Seeking a management position in a dynamic organisation'; you need to be clearer and describe your ideal job. However, make sure you don't go over the top and assign yourself a long list of impressive-sounding adjectives that are either untrue, or which you can't demonstrate in person. Be concise, clear and honest.

EXAMPLE CAREER OBJECTIVE

Position in the broadcasting industry.

This statement is too general.

IMPROVED CAREER OBJECTIVE

A creative self-starter is seeking a position that will make full use of her broad range of experiences as actor, producer and director of a number of school and university theatrical productions. I am looking for a challenging position in the broadcasting industry that will enable me to further my creative skills and organisational experience.

EXAMPLE CAREER OBJECTIVE

Position in a finance organisation.

This statement is too general.

IMPROVED CAREER OBJECTIVE

A highly-motivated economics graduate, I am seeking a position that will fully exploit my experience in finance and cost control. From my internship with a leading accountancy firm, I have a proven ability to define issues, propose solutions and implement changes.

CHOOSE THE RIGHT CV FOR YOUR JOB SEARCH

Because every person is different, you want a CV that presents your skills in the most marketable and attractive light.

It's important to consider carefully which style to use when you apply for a job. A carefully-written, targeted CV will impress a personnel officer far more than a random story of your life.

Knowing how to put together the various types of CV will stand you in good stead as you progress through your career and come across different job opportunities. These days people may have several different careers (not just jobs) during their working lives, so at some stage a non-traditional CV may suit your needs best. Below are the four main types, with some pointers for each one.

Remember to give the most space to the most important facts of your life. If a part-time job or a course module is critical to your application, give it twice as much space as other, less important facts.

Chronological CV

When you are starting off on your career path, looking for your first or second job, this CV—the most popular by far—is probably most appropriate to your experience.

This type of CV also works well as you progress up a standard career ladder. For example, if you begin your career as a junior designer, you move on to become senior designer, and are hoping to become design manager, this is the CV type to use.

1 Write your name and contact details at the top.

2 If you are applying speculatively, state your job search objective clearly.

3 At this early stage in your career, details of your education may be of most interest to potential employers. Unless you have loads of relevant work experience (or if you'd rather not give your grades too much prominence!), list your education at the top of the CV, in reverse chronological order. List any professional qualifications or training you've undertaken separately.

4 Write your work experience and employment history. Start with your present or most recent position, and work backwards.

5 For each position, describe your major duties and achievements, beginning with an action verb (e.g. 'Achieved', 'Increased', 'Won'). Keep to the point and stress what you've achieved.

6 Keep your career goals in mind as you write and, as you describe your duties and achievements, emphasise those which are most related to your desired job.

Make sure you can account for any chronological gaps in your CV—you may get some awkward questions.

Functional CV

As this type of CV focuses on your skills and accomplishments, it could be the better choice if you are concerned that you don't have much work experience. Functional CVs are useful if you are looking for your first professional job, following a less traditional career path or making a fairly major career change.

1 Write your name and contact details at the top.
2 As this type of CV is well suited to people starting out in their careers, you may want to state your job search objective clearly.
3 Write between three to five separate paragraphs, each one focusing on a particular skill or accomplishment, and each one with a relevant heading.
4 List these 'functional' paragraphs in order of importance, with the one most related to your career goal at the top.
5 Within each functional area, emphasise the most relevant accomplishments or results produced.
6 Add in a brief breakdown of your actual work experience after the last functional area, giving dates, employer and job titles only.
7 Include your education in a separate section at the bottom of the CV, again in reverse chronological order.

Using this CV style means that you can include information about your skills and accomplishments without identifying which employer or situation it was connected to. This is especially helpful if you've signed a non-disclosure agreement, in which you undertake not to reveal specific information about a job or project to potential competitors. These are particularly common in high-tech or research companies.

Concentrate on your personal contribution to whatever it is you're writing about and stress achievements and outcomes

Targeted CV

You should use a targeted CV when you know exactly what job you want. It will help you to make an impressive case for a specific job. It is hard work writing this kind of customised CV, especially if you are applying for several jobs, but it can make you and your abilities stand out from all the others in the pile.

1 Begin by brainstorming a list of key points. For example, what have you done that is relevant to your job target? Are you proud of what you have achieved? Think about what you do that demonstrates your ability to work with people.

2   Write your name and contact details at the top.

3   Think carefully about whether you need to include a job search 'objective' here. As this type of CV is best geared to an application for a specific job, you may not need to include one and could use the space more usefully.

4   From your brainstormed list, select between five and eight skills or achievements that are the most relevant to your job target. Make sure that the statements focus on action and results.

5   Briefly describe your actual work experience beneath each skills/achievement item, giving dates, employer and job titles only.

6   Include your education in a separate section at the bottom of the CV, in reverse chronological order.

Don't waffle! Include only relevant information, but take care to explain yourself clearly.

Capabilities CV

If you have a job already and are aiming for a specific job or assignment within your organisation, the best CV to use is the capabilities CV. Again, you must be willing to take the time to customise your CV for the situation.

1   To create a capabilities CV, you first need to learn all you can about the internal job that you are applying for. Try to come up with between five and eight recent achievements that are relevant to this job opening.

2   List your name and contact details at the top.

3   Think carefully about whether you need to include a job search 'objective' here. As this CV type is generally used when applying for a specific job, you may not need to include one and could use the space more usefully.

4   List your five top accomplishments, focusing on actions taken and results achieved that are relevant to the post you are interested in.

5   Write a brief paragraph about any relevant work experience you have had in your current position. If you haven't been at the company for long, you should provide a complete synopsis of

your work experience as described for the targeted CV.

6   List your education separately at the bottom of the CV in reverse chronological order.

If you're e-mailing your CV, give it a sensible name, not just 'CV.doc'.

You shouldn't need to create a CV for each of these types. The only exception is when you have created one of the standard formats (either a chronological or a functional CV) and a unique opportunity comes up for which one of the customised CVs (either a targeted or a capabilities CV) is more suitable.

Your particular job search and career goals are also unique. As you decide which type of CV to prepare, think about whether you plan on staying in the same field long term or whether you might change careers a few years along the line. Are you aiming for a specific job in a specific company or are you on the lookout for something more original and challenging?

Points to bear in mind . . .

Don't try to include every experience you have ever had. Like many people, you may want to tell a potential employer everything you have ever done to try to impress them. A recruiter or employer will be looking for someone who can express him or herself clearly and effectively, so remember to keep it simple, keep to the point and focus on those things that are most likely to get you an interview.

Try to keep your CV down to one page. So many people waffle, ending up with two pages or more, that your one-pager will help you to really stand out from the crowd.

If you haven't had much experience of writing CVs, you may create one that is nothing more than a mixture of job listings, skills and accomplishments. This will only confuse your reader. Rather than leap straight in, work out which type of CV suits your job search or your target vacancy best. Once you've done this, use the points above to create a well-organised, clear résumé of your skills and experiences.

If you're still concerned about your CV, it might be worth visiting your careers adviser. Even if you're already in your first job, careers services will usually provide a free service for several years after graduation.

If you follow these guidelines you will be well on your way to creating the CV that will get you the interview that will lead to your perfect job!

WHERE NEXT?

BBC One Life:
www.bbc.co.uk/radio1/onelife/work/cvs/cvs_intro.shtml
doctorjob.com (for downloadable CVs and advice):
doctorjob.com/JobHuntingEssentials
Total Jobs: **jobs.msn.co.uk/tjmsn/msn.asp**

MAKING AN IMPACT WITH YOUR COVERING LETTER

UNDERSTAND WHY A COVERING LETTER IS IMPORTANT

A carefully-crafted covering letter can demonstrate your primary motivation and personality—and make all the difference to a recruiter's decision to ask you in for interview.

Once you're happy with your CV, the next thing is to make your covering letter equally impressive. While your CV is a formal record of your skills and achievements, your covering letter's job is to tell the recruiter why they should read your CV. It is another opportunity to personalise each application—a vital part of the process.

There are a variety of reasons why you might write a covering letter and send a CV. These include:
✔ responding to an advertisement
✔ following up on meeting someone
✔ letting a potential employer know that you are available for work

Sometimes you will use a different approach. For example:
✔ when you send a letter to enquire whether there are any job openings. In this letter you would ask who you should send your CV to.
✔ if you visited an organisation in person and filled in a job application.
✔ when you apply for a job on the Internet. If you apply online via an agency, you may be asked to fill in a form to accompany your

CV attachment. Often you'll just be asked to give your contact details, but some agencies ask for a brief statement to support your CV.

If you are replying to an advertised job vacancy, a covering letter also gives you the opportunity to include details that the advertisement may have asked for but which can't easily be fitted into a CV format. These could include:

✔ desired salary
✔ preferences for geographical location
✔ dates you will be available for interview (you may want to include these if you are about to go on holiday for a while)
✔ current salary and notice period (if relevant)

If you're applying for a particular position, it's important to say why you're writing. For example, you could start your letter as follows:

I am very interested in the position of Production Assistant as described in your advertisement of 19 September on the *Daily Post* website.

Alternatively, if you're writing following a recommendation from someone already working at, or known to, the company:

I have been given your name by Mary Robertson regarding the position in Human Resources.

If you're approaching an agency to register your CV as part of your search for a job, the letter should describe the type of job you're looking for, the skills you have that would make you an attractive candidate, your current salary (if you have one!), and any preferences you may have in terms of location.

In all cases, a good covering letter can give a sense of who you are that may not come across in a CV. When you come to write your letter, remember to think about its tone, how you are describing yourself and your skills, and also remember to highlight any research you've done into the company or field of work you're interested in.

COVERING LETTERS: SEVEN GOLDEN RULES

Writing a covering letter is a fairly straightforward process, but there are certain steps you need to follow. If you sound both interesting and interested, you are much more likely to get noticed, interviewed and employed!

Rule 1: names are important

Always address your letter to a particular person; letters addressed to 'Dear Sir/Madam' or 'To Whom It May Concern' are usually thrown away. If you are unsure of who to send it to, look on the Internet or ring up and find out a relevant addressee's name and job title. Pay careful attention to detail. It may sounds obvious, but make sure you double-check the following:

- ✔ the addressee's first name and surname
- ✔ their gender
- ✔ their job title
- ✔ the full company name and address

Remember that your CV and covering letter are personal marketing tools. It's also a good idea to double check that the letter is addressed to the correct company.

Rule 2: it's not what you say, it's the way that you say it

You should kick-start your letter with a short introductory paragraph explaining which job you are applying for, where you found out about the position and company and why you have decided to apply.

The main part of your letter should further explain your reasons for applying to that particular organisation and show that you understand the requirements of the role. Beware—recruiters are experts at spotting blanket covering letters. Each and every one needs to be tailored to the specific job and organisation you are applying to.

Take time to show that you've done your homework and that you understand what the company does and what its aims are. Visit the relevant company's website (if it has one) and look at any recent news articles, especially its press releases. You should also read business newspapers and trade magazines. These will give you a sense of any industry issues facing the company you are interested in. They may also have particular information about the goals of your target company.

> To get across the fact that you've read thoroughly and understood the job advertisement, match the language you use in your letter to the advertisement itself. For example, if the job description mentions 'sales executive', refer to that job title rather than using 'sales assistant'.

Rule 3: sell yourself

Make it clear why you are right for the job. Having identified the selection criteria, it is important that you match these with your application and explain why you are right for the job. Again, the reasons you give need to be as relevant as possible, highlighting and elaborating upon achievements in your CV. Be confident but not arrogant. Include information that is not on the CV but is particularly relevant to the role.

> Sell yourself, but be yourself. While CVs are factual records of your experiences and skills, a covering letter is a chance to show your personality and stand out from the crowd. Keep the letter professional, but don't be afraid to show your enthusiasm, your willingness to work hard and your interest in the position. Potential employers want job applicants who seem eager to be a part of their company.

Rule 4: accuracy is important

Covering letters are also a quick and easy way of assessing your writing skills, so the same rules about checking for spelling, grammar or typos still apply—probably more so on your letter. Don't rely on spellcheck or even your own English skills. Get at least one other person to check both your covering letter and CV before you send them.

Use the highest-quality paper that you can afford. Also, unless you are applying for a particularly creative post, use plain paper in ivory or white, and use a standard and easily readable font such as Times New Roman or Arial.

Rule 5: short is sweet

The best advice is to keep your covering letter simple, with a formal yet friendly tone. Remember that, as with your CV, a recruiter will probably have a pile of applications to read through, so you need to make sure your letter is succinct and makes an impact. After all, the easier it is to read and the quicker you get to the point, the more likely you are not to get overlooked. Your letter should be no longer than a page and ideally no more than three or four paragraphs.

End on a positive note, reaffirming both your suitability and enthusiasm for the position. You can be very proactive and finish with, 'I will contact you next week to see how my application is progressing'—but make sure that you do!

You will conduct a more successful job campaign if you combine well-written letters with effective face-to-face and telephone networking.

Rule 6: don't forget to sign your letter

Sounds obvious but you'd be surprised at the number of people who forget!

If you are e-mailing the covering letter and CV, remember to check that you've attached the files before you send the e-mail! Also tell the e-mail recipient what type of file you're attaching and be prepared to send it in another format in case they have difficulty opening it.

Rule 7: follow it up

Not following up an application is the commonest and most serious mistake. If your covering letter says that you will phone to set up an interview, you must note the date down and follow it up. Although fear of rejection can put you off making the call, you will never get the job if you don't!

Your covering letter is, in most cases, your first contact with a prospective employer. There's no time for small talk, no place for rambling—you need to hit the ground running and ensure your letter leads them onto your CV.

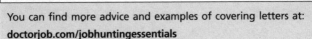

WHERE NEXT?

You can find more advice and examples of covering letters at: **doctorjob.com/jobhuntingessentials**

GETTING TO GRIPS WITH ONLINE APPLICATIONS

THE SAME, ONLY DIFFERENT

In a couple of years, the paper graduate application form will be consigned to the dustbin of history. Applications to all but the smallest organisations will be made online.

But before you go all nostalgic, it's worth remembering what a pain it is (was?) to fill in application forms in your best handwriting. Online applications are still a pain but not such a big one. Nothing fundamental has changed apart from the medium of application.

By placing everything online, companies can make graduates complete competency questionnaires, ability tests, personality profiles and other tests at the beginning of the selection process, rather than having to spend more money and time in bringing them in for an interview.

Exercise caution with e-applications. Watch that you don't ramble and succumb to errors of grammar and spelling. Unhelpfully, most online application forms don't include grammar- and spell-checks so be as careful as you would be on a paper form. Poor spelling and bad grammar are a reason to reject applicants in any medium.

Big benefits

Online systems produce all sorts of useful information on every applicant instantly, and they show people like you that the employer is cutting-edge.

Less obvious, perhaps, are the benefits to you:

✔ You get a rapid response to your application—no more waiting weeks for a letter to arrive.

✔ They're quicker to complete than a paper application form.

✔ Because it's a more objective system, it's fairer. You won't be rejected because your handwriting is awful or the person reading it has had a bad day.

✔ If the forms incorporate a self-assessment test, they allow you to exercise some selection of your own—are they a good choice of organisation, am I really suited to the work?

✔ The better systems give you instant feedback on your application.

✔ They give you another measure of the organisation—how easy is the system to use, have you been treated fairly, can you track your application, is the feedback helpful?

THREE ONLINE APPLICATIONS MYTHS

1   I don't want to send my personal details into cyberspace!
Employers take security extremely seriously and use the very latest technology to ensure that only you and they have access to your personal details. And don't worry about your form getting lost in the ether. It's far more likely to get lost in the Post Office.

2   I don't want to be rejected by a machine.
Although parts of your application will be read by a machine, the decision to invite you for interview (or not) will be taken by a human. A member of the recruitment team will nearly always read the prose parts of your application.

3   I'll be discriminated against because I'm partially sighted.
This is why some organisations are still offering the option of online or traditional application forms. However, if you have any problems with access at college, are visually impaired or have

special needs that prevent you from applying online, give the organisation a call and see how they can help. It's another good way to judge how responsive and flexible they are.

WHAT'S SO DIFFERENT?

The aim of an online application form is the same—to get an interview— but there are a few special bits of advice . . .

If you can, download the form and think about your answers, especially those that require a paragraph or two of your finest prose. Draft it out to your satisfaction before returning to the screen.

Email is a casual form of communication and has bred a shorthand form of written English that is wildly inappropriate for online application forms. You should write online in exactly the same way as you would write on paper forms—direct, punchy, accurate and straight to the reader.

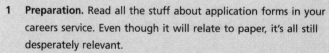

Some organisations use 'key word' searches. If they're particularly keen on leadership and teamwork, their program will spot these words in your application. Don't let this influence you to pepper your prose with too many power words. It will ruin the flow. But equally, it does no harm to describe yourself in the positive language that all organisations like.

Some online application systems include tests as part of the process. See chapter 18 (from p.126) for advice on these.

THE FIVE STAGES OF ONLINE APPLICATIONS

1   **Preparation.** Read all the stuff about application forms in your careers service. Even though it will relate to paper, it's all still desperately relevant.

2   **Data entry.** You will have to register by creating a password that will allow you to come back to your form later. The form itself will consist of a number of factual questions—about your

education and work experience—and more open-ended questions that require longer answers.

3 **Submitting the application.** When you are as happy as you'll ever be, press the submit button. This is the point of no return. Your form arrives at the organisation seconds later.

4 **Data received.** Once your form reaches the organisation it might be automatically scanned or it may be printed off and, ironically, turned back into paper. However it's processed, you'll hear back very quickly with the outcome.

5 **Response.** Because online application systems collect more data about you than conventional forms, you will nearly always get a more reasoned response. Even if it's a rejection, it should be a more helpful rejection.

FAQS

I find it hard to write on screen. Will this be a problem?

Some people can't write easily on screen; you need time to cogitate, anyway. If possible, download the form, take it away and draft your answers.

What happens if the computer crashes halfway through?

This is not a problem, as most systems will automatically be saving your responses as you go along. Even if it crashes in the middle of a test that you can only take once, the technology is sophisticated enough to know what's happened and let you start again.

What's to stop me and my mates sitting round the screen completing the form together?

What's to stop you and your mates sitting round a paper application form doing the same thing? You can do it, of course, but what's the point? Bluffing your way into an unsuitable organisation will only end in tears.

ALL ABOUT . . . APPLICATION FORMS

Applications are no fun. But the more difficult the form, the more people are turned off applying and therefore, the theory goes, it's the motivated candidates that see the job through.

I can't fit my life into this!

Many application forms are designed to test your powers of précis. The size of the space is a guide to how much detail an employer expects; if they give you a small space to comment on your work experience, that's how importantly they view it. The converse, sadly, is true. A large space means a long answer. And if your answer is shorter than the question, it's a fair assumption that the time you've spent on it will be wasted.

Mind the gap(s)

Don't leave gaps in your life. The people who read forms are very experienced at spotting the missing year. Unfortunately, the construction that they will put on the missing time is not that you got the dates wrong but that you have something to hide. It's always a better idea to explain what happened honestly and positively.

Make it a pleasure to read

Considering the sheer number of applications most recruiters receive, it follows that any form which is a) easy to read and b) the product of intelligent thought, will have an immediate advantage. Avoid large passages of unbroken text—whether it's a handwritten or online form. If you have a large space to fill, use headings and/or paragraph spaces.

The odd spelling mistake or bizarre sentence construction may pass unnoticed, but a form that is peppered with mistakes will make you appear careless. It's always safer to get your forms checked by a fresh—and trustworthy—pair of eyes before sending them off.

Choose your referees with care

You will usually be asked for the names of two referees. If you are a student or recent graduate, one of them should have seen you working.

Failing that, you can always ask a family friend who has known you for years. What you must do is to choose reliable people who have agreed to help. Your offer of employment will be subject to receiving references, so nominate referees who won't let you down.

DIFFICULT QUESTIONS

However well you prepare, you will, on the odd occasion, be totally perplexed by certain questions.

That said, there should be no such thing as a difficult question if you have a clear idea of the selection criteria and how they match your skills, knowledge and experience. If you have followed the steps in chapters one and two you should have already made a good start on learning about your marketable skills. Have a go at the questions below.

Questions about you

As most application forms are designed around the organisation's selection criteria, many questions are predictable:

- ✔ Describe a situation where you have had to influence people.
- ✔ Give one or two recent examples to illustrate your ability to work effectively with others.

More difficult are questions about you that seem unrelated to selection criteria:

- ✔ Looking at your life as a whole, indicate three key events or experiences which you consider to have been instrumental in shaping who you are.
- ✔ Identify any major successes in your life to date.

Make sure that the examples you use are drawn from different areas of your life and that you concentrate on your personal contribution to whatever it is you're writing about. Stress achievements and outcomes and the skills, knowledge and insight you gained. Even the most routine summer job can show an employer how you react under pressure, deal with people and solve problems.

Don't forget that flashes of originality will make you stand out.

Questions about the job

Other questions rely on you having made the connection between what they want and what you've got.

✔ What skills and qualities can you bring to our organisation?
✔ Why do you think you would be suited to this career?
✔ Explain which factors attract you to your choice of career.

You will often be asked questions about your suitability for the job or why you have chosen that particular organisation. Don't just list a dozen reasons for your suitability. Think of a limited number—three, maybe four—factors that attract you and go into more detail with supporting evidence.

Then apply the originality test. Look at what you intend to write and decide if 2,000 other people are going to say the same thing. If your answer is predictable, even though it's true, it won't stand out.

Questions about the future

Fortunately this type of question is dying out and it's quite unusual to be asked how you see your future developing. It's no use mapping out a future for yourself that bears no relationship to career progression within that organisation. Use what you know about the organisation and what you know about your own career preferences to describe as detailed a progression as possible. Don't worry—they won't hold you to it!

Biodata questions

These require you to tick a box rather than write an answer. Some deal with factual details like exam grades, technical skills, activities undertaken. These are then optically read and scored.

It's a lot trickier when the biodata questions concentrate on more ambiguous personality factors. One graduate recruitment form has 85 short statements, to each one of which you have to answer: 'either', 'rarely', 'sometimes', 'often', 'most of the time' or 'always'. The statements include the following:

✔ I let matters drop to prevent conflict
✔ I seek out information to back all decisions

The worst thing to do is to think too much. Look at the statements above. If you answer 'rarely' to the first, does that mean you are resolute or just plain stubborn? These personality inventories are impossible to second-guess and your first, honest response is usually the best.

Open-ended questions

Structure is the key here. Don't ramble, and use headings to highlight the different sections of your answer. With these longer questions, the simplest structure to adopt is:

Paragraph 1: say why you are interested in this job with this organisation.

Paragraph 2: describe the key qualities that you can bring to the job (with evidence that proves you have them).

Paragraph 3: detail any work experience or coursework that has been of special relevance.

Paragraph 4: list any relevant technical skills.

FIVE TIPS FOR WINNING APPLICATION FORMS

1   **Read and follow the instructions.** If you don't, your application may be filed in the bin in spite of your match of skills. Answer every question accurately or at least write 'not applicable' so that the recruiter knows you haven't missed it by mistake.

2   **Ensure that your application reflects and reiterates everything you say about yourself.** If you claim to have 'a keen eye for detail', for example, you need to ensure there

are no errors in the finer details on your application form. And remember that applications are often checked to ensure the information is true.

3 **Allow yourself plenty of time.** Print or photocopy the form and work on the copy. Before you start, read through the entire form so that you can plan where to place information, to avoid repeating yourself.

4 **Proofreading after a day or two or getting feedback on what you have written from someone else is well worth the extra time taken.** When you are completely satisfied, send it off. Keep a record of your final answers so you can remind yourself what you wrote if you're called to interview.

5 **Don't leave it until the last moment.** Sending your application in at the last moment doesn't do justice to all your hard work.

WHERE NEXT?

Find advice on every aspect of completing application forms at:
doctorjob.com/jobhuntingessentials
Practise filling in online forms at select simulator:
www.selectsimulator.com/Welcome.asp

SUCCEEDING IN INTERVIEWS

GETTING STARTED

Congratulations! You've cleared the first hurdle in your job search with a great application, and have been invited for an interview—you've already found a way to stand out from the crowd.

Now you need to build on this success. As you prepare yourself for your interview, keep these questions in mind:

- ✔ Why do you think you are the best person for the job?
- ✔ What is it about this job that attracts you?
- ✔ What is it about this organisation that has made you apply for the position?
- ✔ Who will interview you and what do you know about them?
- ✔ What is the appropriate dress and/or image for this organisation?

Do your homework

Review your CV or application form. Remind yourself thoroughly of all the information there. Work through the next chapter and build a stock of answers to potentially tricky questions. Write notes on what you are going to say and practise your answers.

Always have examples ready to back up any claims you make about yourself and your skills.

Look at the company website, focusing on the annual report, news, press releases, and biographies. This will give you a feel for the organisation. If they don't have a website, ring them and ask to be sent this information.

Research current factors that might affect the organisation, such as industry trends, competitive issues, strategic direction and particular challenges or opportunities.

FIVE QUESTIONS TO RESEARCH BEFORE THE INTERVIEW

1   How large is the organisation?
2   How is the organisation structured?
3   What is its main business?
4   Who are its major competitors?
5   What is its work culture?

Decide what you want to get from the interview

Identify the key points you want to make about your strengths and skills. When you prepared your CV, you listed the key strengths and skills that you thought an employer would be looking for. Revisit that list, choose a skill and think of a recent situation you have been in that will highlight it. If possible, include any concrete results achieved due to that particular strength or skill.

It is important to focus on the positive in your answers, even when you have been asked to talk about a difficult situation or your weaknesses. That way you will come across as someone who rises to a challenge and looks for opportunities to improve and develop.

Remember that *you* are also interviewing the organisation, so prepare a list of questions that will help you decide whether or not this job is a good fit for your personality and your career goals.

FIVE KEY QUESTION AREAS TO ASK THE INTERVIEWER

1 What are the company's values?

2 What is the company's success factor?

3 What are the promotion opportunities?

4 What is the company's professional development policy?

5 What does the interviewer think about X [mention a story you have read about that affects the organisation or industry that you are applying to]?

Prepare yourself mentally

Before the interview, visualise yourself being professional, interesting, and enthusiastic in your interview. Also imagine yourself leaving the interview with a good feeling about how you did. This will put you in a positive frame of mind and help you to be at your very best in the interview.

Arrive 15 or 20 minutes early so that you can take some time to relax. Go and freshen up to help you feel more comfortable and confident. Drink some water, flick through company magazines if they are available. Try to get a feel for the atmosphere, as this will help you to decide if it's the sort of place you can see yourself being happy working in. It will also give you an idea of what to expect in the interview, and the sort of candidate the interviewers will be looking for.

Ask a friend or family member to role-play the interview with you. University careers advisers will also do this. Give them a list of questions that you think you might be asked. Role-play the interview and then ask for feedback. Video the role-play if you can, so that you can watch your body language.

SEVEN TYPICAL INTERVIEW QUESTIONS

1 Tell me a little bit about yourself.

2 Where do you see yourself in your career five years from now?

3 What are you most proud of in your experiences to date?

4 What is your greatest strength?

5 What is your biggest weakness?

6   Describe a difficult situation and how you handled it.

7   Can you tell me about a time when you had to be diplomatic?

If you prepare well for an interview by knowing your CV, listing likely questions and responses, researching the company and the people, role-playing the interview and dressing appropriately, you will arrive at the interview feeling confident and enthusiastic. This confidence will help you to make the best impression that you can and you will come away feeling you have done your very best—whatever the outcome.

Don't be over-confident. Never assume the job is yours.

SUCCEEDING IN PANEL INTERVIEWS

When you are looking for a job, sooner or later you may be asked to attend a panel interview.

Although it can be terrifying walking into an interview where several people are present, a panel interview is also an excellent opportunity to show your strengths to a number of interviewers at once. A successful panel interview is one in which you come across cool and confident and able to handle whatever is thrown your way.

FIVE TOP TIPS FOR PANEL INTERVIEWS

1   Do your homework.

2   Answer the questions!

3   Sometimes it can feel as though questions are coming at you from all directions. Answer the first question, then build on that answer to respond to the second interviewer's question. Make sure you answer every question. You do not want one of the interviewers thinking that you ignored his or her question.

4   Clarify questions if necessary. If you find a question confusing, don't be afraid to ask for further explanation. Phrases such as,

> 'Just to clarify...' or, 'If I understand correctly, you want to know...' can help you understand exactly what information the interviewers are looking for.
>
> 5   If you are unsure, check that your answers were understood and that you have answered the question fully. Simply ask the appropriate person, 'Did I answer your question?'

As you are talking, make eye contact with each member of the panel in turn. This means catching the gaze of a particular member of the panel, holding it for about three seconds, and then moving to the next panel member. In reality, it is very difficult to look someone in the eye, count to three, and then move on, all while answering a challenging question. However, this is a very useful skill to use in meetings and public speaking, and will become second nature after a bit of practice.

Don't turn up to interview reeking of booze from the night before!

SUCCEEDING IN TELEPHONE INTERVIEWS

Initial interviews by telephone are becoming more common, but they are quite challenging for both parties.

1   Have everything ready before you start: papers, pen, information you will need to put across accurately, dates, and so on.
2   Make sure you find a quiet room to take the call in, where you won't be interrupted or have any distractions. You may need to refer to some notes, but try not to rustle your papers too much.
3   Watch the tendency to talk too much! Pauses—even very short ones—are awkward on the phone and with no visual cues to guide you it is tempting to fill spaces with words.
4   Take care not to become monotonous—your voice is important

because you cannot make an impression visually. As in any interview sound positive, friendly and business-like.

4   Since you get no visual information on the phone, you should pay careful attention to the non-verbal aspects of speech—tone, pitch, inflection, for example—to pick up clues about what the interviewer is interested in.

6   Make notes of important facts and agreements—it is easy to forget things when you are under pressure.

SUCCEEDING IN COMPETENCE-BASED INTERVIEWS

The idea behind competence-based interviews (often called behavioural interviews) is to determine how well suited you are to a job by ascertaining what you have learnt from situations in the past.

Most interviews incorporate some competence-based questions, because research shows that they seem to be the most effective form of assessment, as your knowledge and experience are being judged against the specific criteria of the job. Competence-based questions usually start with 'Give me an example of when…' or 'Describe a situation where…'

As a rule of thumb, there are certain competences that almost all employers will be interested in. A shortlist of favourites is:

✔ planning and organising
✔ decision making
✔ communicating
✔ influencing others
✔ teamwork
✔ achieving results
✔ leadership

Prepare examples

Given that the interview will focus on past experience, it's useful to think about examples you could use to show how you have developed the core competences listed above.

When you look back at these experiences, ask yourself the following questions:

- ✔ What did you do personally?
- ✔ How did you overcome barriers or pitfalls?
- ✔ What did you achieve?
- ✔ Is there anything you would have done differently?
- ✔ What did you learn from the experience?

While you may not be asked precisely these questions, they will prepare you for areas of questioning you are highly likely to encounter in the interview.

SUCCEEDING IN 'HYPOTHETICAL' OR SCENARIO-BASED INTERVIEWS

Most interviewers have been carefully trained to look only for evidence and facts from the candidate's past and therefore never to ask hypothetical questions. But sometimes—especially with candidates without much past work experience—an organisation will be more interested in what the person can become in the future than in what he or she is now.

There are techniques for doing this. They normally focus on exploring how you think and act when confronted with problems you haven't experienced before—*how* rather than *what* you think and do. The logic is that in order to learn from a new experience you must be able to understand the experience thoroughly. These interviews assess the level of complexity at which you can think—and therefore understand the issues and learn how to deal with them.

Typically, you'll be asked in these interviews to take part in a conversation that gets more complex and wide-ranging as it progresses. You build a scenario further and further into the future. There are no right answers, of course; the interviewer is looking for an ability to spot the right questions.

Knowing that the interview will take this form is some help, but there is really little that you can do to prepare for it. Being well-rested and alert, and relaxing and enjoying the challenge are the best tips.

SUCCEEDING IN STRESS INTERVIEWS

This is where you're deliberately put under pressure to see how you respond to difficult people or unexpected events.

Organisations should only use this technique when they can clearly show the need for it, and even then they should be careful how it is handled, taking account of the sensitivities of the interviewee. It can be an unnerving experience, but being aware that this is a recognised interviewing technique for some firms will help you to cope should you come across it. The sorts of industries that may employ this technique include banking and some security firms.

Stress questions often come in the form of role play, when the interviewer, *in his or her role*, may say something like: 'I think your answer is totally inadequate: it doesn't deal with my concerns at all. Can't you do better than that?' The interviewer is testing your ability to manage surprises and ambiguity. He/she will want to see you keep the initiative and take responsibility for dealing with the situation appropriately.

The trick is not to take the remarks personally but to recognise that you are required to play a role. Take a deep breath, pause, keep your temper and respond as naturally and accurately as you can.

Keep your wits about you because the technique is designed to catch you off guard. Create time for yourself to balance logic and emotion calmly in framing your response.

Try to anticipate what the next problem will be and keep ahead of the game.

Carry yourself confidently from the moment you arrive until after you've left.

SUCCEEDING IN TECHNICAL INTERVIEWS

This is where you are asked specific questions relating to technical knowledge and skills.

Technical interviews are common in research and technology companies' selection processes. The organisation will normally tell you in advance that they have a technical interview or if they want you to give a presentation on your thesis or experience. You need to be prepared for 'applied' questions that ask for knowledge in a different form from the way you learned it at college.

For example, 'How would you design a commercially viable wind turbine?' or 'How would you implement the requirements of data protection legislation in a small international organisation?'

Consider the 'audience' and how your knowledge fits with their likely interests and priorities. What questions are they likely to ask?

Sometimes these presentations go wrong when interviewers ask very 'obvious' questions; or one of them has a favourite or 'trick' question. It is easy to be irritated by these, but you should remain calm and courteous. Try to see the interviewers as your 'customer' and respond with patience.

As always, preparation and anticipation are the keys to success. Work out what your interviewers will want to know and make sure your knowledge is up to scratch in the correct areas.

WHERE NEXT?

Visit doctorjob.com for practical advice to help you succeed in interviews: **doctorjob.com/jobhuntingessentials**

HANDLING TRICKY INTERVIEW QUESTIONS

GETTING STARTED

Job interviews are the single most important part of the work selection process—for you and for your future employer.

Once your CV has shown that you meet the basic skills and background requirements, the interview then establishes how well you might fit into an organisation's culture and future plans.

Most interview questions are generally straightforward, unambiguous inquiries, but some interviewers like to surprise you by asking questions specifically intended to explore your thinking and expectations. Or they might try to throw you off guard to see how you react in high-stress or confusing circumstances. Or they may not be intentionally tricky at all. The interviewer may not be very experienced and so ask you questions which seem unrelated to you and the position. Don't let this throw you!

Answering tricky questions successfully could help you to gain the position, but remember that the nature of the questions, and how your answers are received, can tell you volumes about whether this is a company you would actually *want* to work for.

BE PREPARED

Spend time in advance thinking about questions you might be asked.

Questions that might be difficult to answer include, 'Why did you choose to study this subject?' or 'What did you do during that vacation?'.

Go through the list of eight question topics below, study lists of questions that are available online and formulate possible answers. Although you may not be asked those questions specifically, being well prepared will help you feel relaxed, confident, and capable—exactly what the interviewer is looking for!

✔ What specific skills and knowledge can you bring to this job?
✔ What are your strengths, and how can you make sure they are discussed in the interview?
✔ What are your weaknesses? Do you feel especially worried about discussing them? Formulate answers to questions about your weaknesses in advance.
✔ How can you use the interview to learn about the potential employer?

Think about the purpose

The best job interviews are polite encounters that allow a two-way exchange of information. It may feel as though the employer has all the power as it is they who will decide whether or not to offer you the job. But, in fact, it is *you* who holds the power—it is *you* who will decide whether or not to accept the job. So interviews are just as important for you as they are for the interviewer.

Keeping this power balance in mind will help you to stay calm, dignified and clear-headed.

Think about the interviewer

It is safe to assume that the interviewer is slightly uncomfortable with the process too. Not many people enjoy grilling a stranger.

Remember that you may be the 25th candidate, and the interviewer may be quite sick of asking the same old questions and hearing the same rehearsed answers. Remember, too, that the interviewer was once sitting in your seat, applying for his or her job in the company and worrying about the same surprise questions.

Empathising with the interviewer will help you to break down any barriers.

| **THREE TIPS FOR COMMUNICATING EFFECTIVELY IN INTERVIEW** |

1   **Never lie.** Many interviewers do this work for a living; they have heard all the 'correct' answers many times before. Don't trot out what you think they want to hear. Instead, be candid and clear, and use lengthy answers only when you think that demonstrating your thought processes in detail will add valuable information.

2   **Be sure you understand the question.** If the question is unclear, ask for clarification. 'I'm not sure what you mean. Could you explain?' or 'Could you rephrase that question?' are perfectly acceptable queries in any civilised conversation. Job interviews are no different.

3   **Be prepared to answer questions about salary.** Declining—however politely—to give details about salary and expectations can create a bad atmosphere. Decide ahead of time on an acceptable salary range, and remember that the important thing is to keep the focus on your *worth*, not your *cost*. See chapter 20 (from p.137) for guidance on negotiating your package.

BE PREPARED FOR TRICKY QUESTIONS

Here are the most likely areas of questioning that could pose a challenge in the interview:

1   your experience and skills
2   your opinions on industry or professional trends
3   the financial or other value of your past achievements
4   your work habits
5   your salary expectations
6   your expectations for the future
7   your personality and relationship skills or problems

You may be faced with an interviewer who doesn't seem to know why certain questions are being asked—they may be from an outside employment agency. In this case, help them, and yourself, by exploring the reasons why the question might be included and what exactly is being looked for in the way of response. This will show that you are not easily rattled and that you can work calmly and cooperatively towards a solution.

Identify the topic areas that might be the trickiest for you, then think carefully about how you might answer them. You don't want to have to try to blag your way through difficult parts of the interview, and you certainly shouldn't lie. But you also shouldn't rehearse answers to anticipated questions word for word, as this will come across as false and insincere.

Your solutions to 'scenario' type problems will tell the interviewer a lot about you—whether you can make tough decisions, for example, or if you have leadership qualities. Try to answer these kinds of questions based on business strategy.

Questions about your weaknesses are usually designed to discover the extent of your self-knowledge. Keep your answer short and dignified. Identify only one area of weakness that you're aware of, and describe what you are doing to strengthen that area. Try to avoid using the response of being a 'perfectionist' as it is a cliché. Remember, no-one is perfect.

When you are talking about past experiences and giving examples of your work, don't use the royal 'we' (e.g. 'we did this' or 'we did that'). Use 'I'. This will reflect better upon you even when you are talking about weaknesses, as it demonstrates self-knowledge and the confidence to take responsibility for the decisions you've made.

FOUR COMMON INTERVIEW MISTAKES

1   **Getting angry or defensive.** A job interview is part gamesmanship, part blind date, part tea party! Use your social skills to smooth over any uncomfortable moments, and try not to bristle at questions you find offensive. And don't take anything personally.

2   **Thinking interviews are one-sided.** Remember, you are at the interview to find out how desirable the job is to you, just as much as to sell your own desirability to the company. This thought will help you to keep your dignity and prevent you from feeling you must answer inappropriate, irrelevant or intrusive questions.

3   **Criticising former employers or colleagues.** Focus on your positive ambitions, not any resentments or grudges from previous jobs. Talk about what has worked in your career to date, not what has failed.

4   **Using scripted answers to anticipated questions.** Scripted answers are artificial, and the interviewer has heard them all before. Original responses, even if they are slightly clumsy, will be more valuable both to you and the interviewer. They are a more accurate guide as to whether there is indeed a match between you and your potential employer.

DEALING WITH INAPPROPRIATE QUESTIONS IN INTERVIEW

BE PREPARED

Occasionally, you may be interviewed by someone who asks inappropriate questions. These may just put you in a difficult position—or they may fall into the category of 'politically incorrect'.

Even though most interviewers are very professional and well trained in appropriate interviewing techniques, you should still work out a strategy to deal with this situation—just in case.

There are two steps in preparing to handle inappropriate questions: deciding what is inappropriate or uncomfortable to you, and deciding how you will respond.

Think about the issues below as they will help you to be ready to deal with inappropriate questions:

- ✔ What kinds of question would feel inappropriate to me?
- ✔ If I get asked this kind of question, what does that say about the organisation I am applying to?
- ✔ How could I deal with inappropriate questions?

Find out which interview questions are unlawful

The worst types of inappropriate questions are actually unlawful. Legislation has been put in place to ensure employers make their selection decisions based on fair and objective criteria and to assess your suitability for the job they must avoid asking unfairly discriminatory questions. This legislation can be extremely complicated, and is often reviewed and modified, but helpful resources are the Advisory, Conciliation and Arbitration Service and the Citizens Advice Bureau (see **Where next?**). You can read more on equal opportunities in chapter 24, on p.164.

Very few UK websites will tell you directly which questions are unlawful and which aren't because of the great complexity of the issue, but they can help you to determine whether or not you have been discriminated against during a job interview (or, indeed, at any stage in your career).

Inappropriate interview questions

Any question which does not relate directly to your ability to do the job may be considered inappropriate. Some questions that ask about personal circumstances may be unfairly discriminatory if your answers are taken into account when your potential employer makes their selection of the successful candidate. Examples of such questions in the United Kingdom might be:

✔ Those which ask about family circumstances, such as:
  • Do you have a boyfriend/girlfriend/partner?
  • Are you single, married or divorced?
  • Are you planning to start a family?
  • Do you have any children? How old are they?
  • Will your partner/husband/wife move if we offer you this job?

✔ Those which refer to your ability to carry out the role with regard to your gender, race, age and sexuality, such as:
  • How would you feel working for a white female boss?
  • Why would a woman want a job like this?
  • How will you cope with all the travel bearing in mind you're confined to a wheelchair?
  • How will you cope with speaking to customers on the phone with English as your second language?

Note that there are some questions about personal circumstances, such as physical ability, previous convictions, or religion that might not necessarily be discriminatory. Before responding, it's important to understand the reasons why you are being asked the question to enable you to target your response in a suitable and professional way.

Draw up your boundaries

Make a list of interview questions that would feel inappropriate to you. These might be questions about your personal life, or about what you enjoy doing after work. It is up to you to decide if the question is inappropriate to you.

For example, imagine your CV says you spent time in Brazil. The interviewer asks, 'What was your favourite thing to do at the weekends in Brazil?' This question is not work-related, but it probably won't make you feel uncomfortable. You may answer that you enjoyed swimming at weekends, and so the interviewer tells you that this organisation has a swimming club. On the other hand, you may have worked as a volunteer for an AIDS organisation, and you may not wish to discuss your reasons for doing this. In this case, the question might feel inappropriate to you.

FIVE REASONS WHY THE INTERVIEWER MIGHT ASK A SEEMINGLY INAPPROPRIATE QUESTION

1 **Ice-breaking.** In some instances you might feel that the interviewer is trying to be friendly and asking you some nice easy questions to 'break the ice'.

2 **Nerve-calming.** If the interviewer can see you are tense and nervous during the interview, he or she may change tack and ask you some questions about your hobbies or likes and dislikes to get you back onto familiar territory.

3 **Bonding.** The interviewer might identify with something you have written on your application form or CV, e.g. 'active member of local Christian society' and want to find some common ground.

4 **Poor interviewing technique.** You may be being interviewed by someone who is unskilled in the etiquette of interviewing and he or she may not realise that question is inappropriate.

5 **Deliberate discrimination.** In some circumstances, your interviewer may be asking a question designed to assess your suitability for the job based on unlawful or inappropriate criteria.

KNOW HOW TO RESPOND TO INAPPROPRIATE QUESTIONS

Never let an interviewer intimidate you by asking inappropriate questions. You have a right to be treated professionally and with dignity.

There are different ways you can answer:

✔ **Clarification.** Check that you have understood the question, by asking them to clarify what they are asking: 'I'm not sure I understand your question, could you rephrase it for me?' This also gives your interviewer an opportunity to rephrase the question if it was clumsily posed the first time.

✔ **Gentle confrontation.** This generally means asking the interviewer, 'I'm not sure why you're asking me that. Would you mind explaining the reason for asking the question so that I can give you a proper answer?'

✔ **Compliance.** Answer the question.

✔ **Avoidance.** Ignore the question and change the subject.

✔ **Humour.** Respond to the question as if it were a joke, giving the interviewer an opportunity to save face and to ask more appropriate questions.

✔ **Strong confrontation.** Tell the interviewer that the question is inappropriate and that you are not going to answer it—but always clarify that you've understood the question and the reason behind it first!

Decide which response best fits your situation by considering these questions:

✔ Why do you think the interviewer is asking the question?
✔ How intrusive or outrageous is the question?
✔ Can you see why this question relates to the job you have applied for?
✔ How strongly do you want the job?
✔ Is this kind of question a reflection of the corporate culture?

Your answers will help you to decide whether the question is actually fairly harmless and can be safely ignored, or whether the interviewer's behaviour crosses ethical lines and must be confronted. If you *really* want the job, you may decide to overlook the question. If the question is so offensive that you know you could never work for this company, you may be more confrontational.

If you find interview questions really insulting, think hard about whether you really want to work for this company after all.

If you are a woman, a young person or from a minority ethnic group there is a greater chance that you may be asked inappropriate questions. It's a good idea to investigate common areas where inappropriate questions are asked so that you don't jump to the wrong conclusion or end up being discriminated against. If you feel certain that you have been discriminated against during an application, get a second opinion from a lawyer.

TWO TRICKY INTERVIEW MISTAKES

1   **Wanting the job so much that you end up answering a question you feel you shouldn't have been asked.** If this happens, you will leave the interview feeling embarrassed, angry or ashamed. To avoid feeling this desperate when you are job hunting try to line up several exciting interviews. Also spend

> time preparing yourself mentally for the interview, so that you feel a sense of self-worth and self-esteem when you walk into the interview.
>
> 2 **Overreacting to the inappropriate question.** Some may see every comment as a potential insult and leap to conclusions about why a particular question was asked. The result is that the candidate is unlikely to get the job. If you feel yourself overreacting, remember to check you have done your best to make an accurate assessment of the situation and keep in mind that there are better places to fight your battles—a job interview is probably not the best place to make a point about your political values!

Remember that you are not forced to answer any questions in an interview that make you feel uncomfortable. Be prepared: know in advance what you feel is an inappropriate question and have a possible response ready. This will help prevent you overreacting and adding to an already tense situation, and will give you the confidence to make the best of an interview which might otherwise be going well.

WHERE NEXT?

The Advisory, Conciliation and Arbitration Service (ACAS): **www.acas.org.uk**

Citizens Advice Bureau: **www.citizensadvice.org.uk**

Emplaw.co.uk: **www.emplaw.co.uk/free/4frame/index.htm**

Prospects.ac.uk: **www.prospects.ac.uk**

University of Nottingham Staff and Educational Development Unit: **www.nottingham.ac.uk/sedu/recruitment/legal/index.php**

SUCCEEDING
AT ASSESSMENT
CENTRES

GETTING STARTED

Assessment centres usually involve a group of candidates performing different tasks and exercises over the course of one to three days. They were traditionally used at the second stage of recruitment, but nowadays it's not uncommon to be asked to attend one at the first stage.

Organisations that use assessment centres tend to design their own, but many of them will contain similar elements. These can include group exercises, a presentation, a series of aptitude tests or a case study linked to the job function that you have applied for.

Because they give you the opportunity to shine in a variety of settings, assessment centres are a much more accurate way of choosing between individuals. The advantage is that if you do not perform well on one of the exercises, you can compensate for it in another; you have the opportunity to demonstrate a range of skills, not just your effectiveness at being interviewed.

THE GOOD NEWS ABOUT ASSESSMENT CENTRES . . .

✔ You're very close to a job. Especially if it's after an initial interview, as you're safe in the knowledge that most of the competition has disappeared.

✔ You are employable—selection centres are expensive, so everyone who gets an invite is up to the job.

✔ You can mess up occasionally as long as you're OK overall. So they're fairer than interviews.

. . . AND THE BAD NEWS

✔ You are going to have to find out even more about the organisation before you get there.
✔ You may have to do a presentation
✔ You can't drink like a fish, even if the drink is free.

Assessment centres usually include:

✔ **group exercises**, such as:
- role-playing
- discussion
- leadership exercises

✔ **individual exercises,** such as:
- written tests (such as report writing based on case studies)
- in-tray exercises (a business simulation where you are expected to sort through an in-tray, making decisions about how to deal with each item)
- presentation of an argument or data analysis
- psychometric tests
- interviews

✔ **social events**
✔ **company presentations**

You will be assessed most of the time—the administrator should clarify this for you—so there's rarely an opportunity to let down your guard.

FIVE TIPS FOR ASSESSMENT CENTRE SUCCESS
1 **Read any information the organisation sends you.** This will help you to work out what they are interested in.
2 **Behave naturally but thoughtfully.** Do not attempt to play an exaggerated role—it is never what the assessors want to see!

3   **Make sure that you take part fully in all activities.** Assessors can only appraise what you show them.
4   **Don't be over-competitive.** In a group of eight people, it's possible that all of you might get a job offer—or you may all be rejected. You're being assessed against the organisation's criteria, not against the other candidates; unnatural behaviour quickly becomes inappropriate and boorish.
5   **Don't rush in; stand back and look at things in context.** With the in-tray exercise, for example, you will probably find that some items are related and need to be tackled together. Most of the exercises have a purpose wider than the obvious.

What they are looking for

Your assessors will be looking at your social skills (how well you work with others, how you influence and persuade, how others respond to you), which are much easier to observe in a group setting. Employers want to know who you are and what you can do in a given situation, much like you would within the job itself. You need to be aware, flexible and re-active. Turning up with an open mind and a can-do attitude is important, but standard preparation also applies.

'We are disappointed when a candidate comes to an assessment day, but has not even visited one of our stores!'
Claire McBride, resourcing manager for Mothercare

Your careers service can help

Careers services vary, but most will run some sort of practice session for assessment centres. Sometimes recruiters even pay students to act as guinea pigs for new assessment centre formats—events that tend to be coordin-ated by the careers service. It's not great money, but it's fantastic ex-perience and will leave you considerably less emotionally scarred than volunteering for sleep-deprivation and alcohol-indulgence experiments in the psychology department.

A DIARY OF AN ASSESSMENT CENTRE

Based on feedback from recruiters and graduate jobseekers, this is a diary of one candidate's day at an assessment centre.

9.30 Met other candidates. 10 altogether. All look nervous but secretly smug too. Checked each other out surreptitiously. Ominous appearance of people with clipboards.

10.00 Group discussion. Five people in a group. Given 30 minutes for two problems, e.g. production problems related to possible disciplinary action of two employees. One bloke really got on everyone's nerves by trying to speak the loudest and longest.

10.30 Fact-finding exercise. 10 minutes to read a scenario. 20 minutes individually asking questions to one assessor while another took notes. The hardest exercise for me.

11.00 Feedback on progress so far from a selector. Really useful.

11.30 Interview. Criteria-based and quite standard. No tricky questions at all.

12.00 Numerical test. No calculator allowed, but can use scrap paper to work out answers. Brought back bad memories of GCSE maths.

12.30 Case study exercise. Individually analyse a huge pile of information relating to possible projects and human resource allocation. Given time to prepare presentation for afternoon. Common sense but daunting.

13.30 Lunch. Chatted to recent graduates to distract myself from stress about presentation. Lots of much-needed caffeine.

14.30 Case study presentation. 10 minutes with one assessor. Not as bad as I'd thought.

14.45 Group exercise. Choose which event to sponsor as a company. Half an hour to prepare individual case. One hour to discuss as a group. We all had to compromise. That bloke got up everyone's nose again.

16.45 Presentation by company 'big wigs'. Impressive despite my tiredness.

17.15 Taken out for drinks and nibbles. Didn't overdo it at the free bar. Had a chat with some of the other candidates. Presentation by recent star graduates. With any luck I'll be in their shoes next year.

18.30 Home. Exhausted.

GROUP EXERCISES

The purpose of the group exercise is to see your communication and problem-solving skills in action, and to ensure that you can work effectively in a team.

TWO GOLDEN RULES OF GROUP EXERCISES

1   By your actions and words, you must help the group to complete the task.

2   By your actions and words, you must promote your own cause.

A common mistake is to storm in with all guns blazing and dominate the group. Will this get you noticed? Most definitely. Will this get you hired? No. Similarly, an introvert may listen but not contribute, which will not impress either. The best way to impress is to show yourself as a good team player—flexible, full of ideas but willing to listen to and help expand the ideas of others.

The discussion group

A discussion group involves the group members sitting round in a circle and being given a topic or topics to discuss. The nature of the topics can vary but usually they involve an issue of current importance to students or something that's been in the news recently. You are not usually given time to prepare, so it's a good idea to read a quality newspaper in the weeks before the assessment centre.

The leaderless task

This involves each member of the group being given an individual briefing document which may or may not be different from other people's. As a group you must come up with a decision acceptable to all within the time limit. No-one in the group is designated leader so the group has to find a compromise solution.

The leadership task

Very occasionally, you will be asked to chair a meeting or act as leader of your group. Once again there will be a set task but this time you will be expected to be in charge and to lead the others to success. It's worth knowing what is expected of you:

- ✔ A good leader delegates. The task can't be done by you alone; you must divide the work between yourself and the others.
- ✔ A good leader uses the strengths of others. You must identify the strengths of the individuals in your group and use them in appropriate ways.
- ✔ A good leader knows what's going on. Don't get too involved in doing things. It's better to monitor what's going on and make changes if things don't work out.

The job-related scenario

Perhaps the most common group exercise of all is the job-related scenario. Here they want to see how well you operate in a task that approximates to the job area that you have applied for. In nearly every case, you will each be given a different briefing document from the other candidates. The group then has to reach a decision despite the conflicting views of its members.

The ice-breaker

Organisations use ice-breakers to help you relax and to help the group to gel. Sometimes they are practical and involve the completion of a task within a tight deadline, or they might be more intellectual. Everyone is expected to play a part and share information.

SIX TIPS FOR SHINING IN GROUP EXERCISES
1   Use people's names when you are talking to them.
2   Bring people into the discussion.
3   Don't try to be a leader unless you have been given the role.
4   Don't directly criticise someone for their view.
5   Talk to the other candidates and the assessors before and between exercises
6   If you believe in something, express yourself without appearing overbearing or arrogant.

HOW TO BEHAVE

It may still be an unnatural situation, but assessment centres do offer you the chance to show your true self.

Get stuck in. You might be asked to do some strange things, to take part in seemingly irrelevant exercises that you wouldn't do even under the influence of several pints. Don't stand back. Don't turn your nose up. Get stuck in. These exercises are designed to see how well you work with others. In the world of work you will have to work with other people; the assessors just want to make sure that you can.

Watch out for people with clipboards. Throughout the group exercises, you will be watched carefully by assessors with clipboards. They will be noting down the times when you provide either positive or negative examples of their selection criteria. It's easy to be self-conscious when you know that people are watching you, but try to ignore them and try not to read too much into how often or how much they write.

Don't lose concentration. It's only natural that, over the course of the day, your concentration will waver. You might, for example, find yourself overdoing the food and the drink at lunch (or the dreaded 'getting to know you' drinks in the evening) and behaving in a slightly more robust way than you should. Even if they assure you that the informal food and drinks do not play any part in the selection process, it's safe to assume that if you let your hair down too far, someone will notice.

Remember: quality not quantity. Anxiety makes us all behave in strange ways. In group selection, it often makes us want to talk at great length in order to be noticed. And you will be noticed; you will be noticed as the person who never shuts up. Better by far to choose your moment and speak when you have something to say.

Complete the task. Failure to complete the task within the time has serious consequences for the entire group. At the start of the exercise you will always be told how long you have. If no-one else says anything, offer to keep an eye on the time. During the exercise, give the group occasional time-checks. Don't, however, become just the group's timekeeper. You do have to take a full part in the action too.

Never seek to destroy. You will sometimes encounter another candidate who manifests seriously antisocial behaviour. This could involve trying to dominate the group by talking loudly, being dismissive of other people's contributions or mixing exclusively with the assessors. At times like these you must trust the people watching to draw the same conclusions as you. Resist the irresistible temptation to attack them in the group. Disagree by all means, but do it calmly and logically.

Don't act a part. Having studied an organisation's selection criteria, it's easy to convince yourself that you need to come across, for example, much more assertively than normal. This can lead you to behave unnaturally and, unless you are a brilliant actor, your audience, without knowing exactly why, will notice that something is very odd. So be yourself—but be the most positive version of yourself.

WHERE NEXT?

Jobsite: **www.jobsite.co.uk/career/advice/assessment.html**
Prospects:
**www.prospects.ac.uk/cms/ShowPage/Home_page/Applications_and
_interviews/Interviews/Assessment_centres/p!egFlLd**

18

UNDERSTANDING PSYCHOMETRIC TESTS

GETTING STARTED

More and more organisations are using psychometric tests (also known as aptitude tests) to provide them with the sort of information about you that they can't easily get from the rest of the assessment centre.

Psychometric tests are there to give a quantifiable measurement of your mental ability. These can include personality tests but are usually to do with cognitive ability—such as verbal or numerical reasoning—and ensure that you meet basic requirements. Psychometric tests are also often used to help in career guidance and counselling.

Although you can't practise for a personality test (never has the phrase 'just be yourself' been more apt), you can, thankfully, practise a range of different aptitude tests. See **Where next?** at the end of this chapter for some handy links.

WHAT ARE THE DIFFERENT PSYCHOMETRIC TESTS?

Personality tests

These tests are becoming increasingly used by graduate recruiters. They measure your personal preferences and ability to learn new skills, and reveal how much of a certain characteristic you possess, such as motivation, sociability, resilience and emotional adjustment. You can't really 'revise' for these tests; but as they are based on self-awareness, the better you know yourself, the more likely it is that the results will be useful to you.

The questions will ask you to say how you respond to a variety of situations by choosing from a list of possibilities. You may find that they ask very similar questions several times over to judge the fine detail of your responses, and in many cases to check that you are answering straightforwardly and not trying to create a particular impression!

Most of these tests involve multiple-choice answers and provide a numerical score. A higher score is not always 'better', as they often measure multiple skills; a personality test enables employers to see whether you match their ideal profile.

Another type of personality test, **interest inventories** are designed to find out where your career interests lie and the areas of work at which you are likely to be most successful. You will find them being used for career guidance in any careers service office, in some selection processes and for later development of people within an organisation.

Values questionnaires explore collections of values that are relevant to the workplace, such as Achievement, Order and Belonging.

Attainment tests

These are designed to find out how much you know—much like school exams. If you are applying for your first 'real' job you might be confronted with a test of maths, English, or IT skills, for example. They do have 'right answers', so it's important to practise. There are hundreds of test preparation books available.

General intelligence tests

This group of tests, and the next, are concerned with your ability to learn new skills. Intelligence tests measure your capacity for abstract thinking and reasoning in particular contexts. The items usually cover numerical, verbal, and symbolic reasoning, often in the familiar forms, such as: 'What is the missing number in this series...?' The tests in most common use are the AH series, Raven's Matrices, and NIIP tests. The first two have 'advanced' forms for use with graduates and managers.

Special aptitude tests

Some types of work clearly require you to have—or be able to learn—particular skills at a high level. This group of tests is designed to reveal general or specific aptitudes that the employer needs to develop. You may also encounter these tests as part of an online application system. The more common tests include:

- ✔ **Verbal ability,** testing verbal comprehension, usage and critical evaluation.
- ✔ **Numerical ability,** testing numerical reasoning or analysis of quantitative data. You might meet the NA series of tests, NC2, or the GMA numerical test.
- ✔ **Spatial ability,** relating to skill at visualising and manipulating three-dimensional shapes, for example. Frequently used tests are the ST series.
- ✔ **Analytical thinking,** assessing the way in which candidates can read and process complex arguments. These tests are very common among graduates and those applying for MBAs. An example is the Watson-Glaser Critical Thinking test.
- ✔ **IT aptitude.** There are various tests for technical programming ability and word processing.
- ✔ **Sales aptitude.** Tests the special skills and attitudes needed for selling.
- ✔ **Manual dexterity** tests test special manipulation or hand-eye coordination linked to the special requirements of a job. If you are applying for a modern apprenticeship, especially in engineering or technology, you may meet these.
- ✔ **Leadership.** While most of the personality inventories have a leadership dimension, there are some specialised tests, such as LOQ, that focus on leadership behaviours like planning, communication and implementing ability.

Though not widely accepted in the UK, many European employers use graphology, and sometimes astrology as means of appraising personal characteristics. If you are asked to hand-write your application letter the former is probably being used.

TEST-TAKING SKILLS

Read the instructions very carefully. Make sure you understand them completely. Don't be afraid to ask for clarification from the person administering the test. Many people dive right into the test, and so get a much lower score than they deserve because they missed some important information.

For example, in some tests, unanswered questions do not count against you. The instructions may tell you that wrong answers will be subtracted from right answers to provide a final score for the test. In this case, you should skip over questions where you're not sure of the answer—don't just guess. Some tests are timed and, if so, it's important to know how much time you have left so you can focus on the questions that you are most likely to answer correctly.

Remember that different companies will administer tests in different ways. You may find yourself taking the test on your own or in a roomful of other people. Not everyone in there will necessarily be applying for the same job as you, however; some companies hold 'testing days' in which they test all applicants for all vacancies at the same time.

Reflect on the results

If you are taking a test for career guidance, take the results as an indicator—extra information to add to what you already know about yourself. Think carefully about the results but remember that no test is completely accurate, and no-one knows you better than you do yourself. If the career advice provided by the test seems too far off the mark, trust your intuition. You may want to take a different kind of career test as a second opinion.

If you are taking an attainment or aptitude test as part of a job application, the organisation should give you an indication of how you did, even if they don't give you more detailed results. For some companies, that indication may be an invitation to interview. In any case, you have the right to ask for feedback if you have any questions about the whole process. If you have questions about your results you should contact the Human Resources department, who will usually run the whole process.

FOUR COMMON TEST-TAKING MISTAKES

1   **You make a major career shift based on your test results.** Test results are meant to be used for guidance and should only be part of a comprehensive career-planning process. This process should include self-assessment exercises, plenty of personal soul searching, talking to trusted friends and family, and talking things through with your careers adviser.

2   **You don't take the test seriously.** Even though the results can be taken with a pinch of salt, you should adopt a serious attitude towards taking the test. Organisations that use testing often use the results at the very beginning of the recruitment process. If you don't pass, you will not even be considered for an interview. If there *is* a test, be as prepared as possible to do it and to do it well.

3   **You take the test *too* seriously.** It's easy to get worked up, but the fact is that these tests can have such a varied predictive validity that some are only slightly better than chance. Don't feel you've failed if tests don't go to plan, and remember that the company is measuring itself as well as you.

4   **You stay up all night, cramming for the test.** This, and a lot of caffeine, may have been how you got yourself through tests and exams before, so perhaps it has become the way you tackle all tests. But it wasn't a good strategy then, and it's not a good strategy now.

Psychometric tests may seem scary, but they're not. They're not like A levels and GCSEs, where you need to show off what you've learned. Instead they ask you to use your natural abilities. It's a way of showing you have the skills needed to do the job. You'll perform better if you're not nervous. To become familiar with the test situation and to find out just how the tests are made up, do some practice tests.

HOW DO YOU PREPARE FOR TESTS?

Facing a psychometric test? Don't panic! To get the most out of your assessment, you just need to be prepared. Find out what tests you'll be doing, and practice. Even if there are no specific practice questions there are other ways of getting practice. Be prepared so that when you do the real test you'll be cool, calm and collected.

Practice makes perfect

By practicing you will familiarise yourself with the format, improve on speed and become aware of any areas you need to work on. On top of the resources available on the internet, your careers service will probably have books, and your invitation to the testing process may include some practice questions. You don't need to practise for personality tests, though you might like to try some for your own interest. They are usually untimed, so don't rush. There are no right or wrong answers. Don't try to guess which answers the employer wants: there are built-in checks to guard against this. Answer the questions truthfully, but don't over-think your answers as your initial response will be the most accurate representation of yourself. If you're the perfect person for the job, you'll get it.

On the clock

The key is to strike a balance between speed and accuracy. Don't go so fast that you start making mistakes but don't be so careful over each answer that you only get one third of the way through the test. Practice, and you'll find the speed that works best for you. Some tests are designed to put you under pressure to see how well you cope. Don't be put off—just answer as many questions as you can.

All the time in the world

Some tests have no time limit—you can take as long as you want! In these tests you will find that the questions get harder as you go through. The aim is to see how far you get and stop when the questions get too difficult. As speed is not an issue, it's worth taking your time to think carefully over the questions. However, it may be less advisable to miss questions out to return to later—the earlier questions are easier and may help 'build you up' to solve the later questions.

On the day . . .

Make sure you get a good night's sleep before the test, and leave plenty of time to get to the test centre. Bring everything you might need, such as glasses or contacts, a hearing aid or an inhaler. Wear a watch so you can keep track of the time. If you have a disability, let the employer know ahead of time so they can make appropriate arrangements.

> Be physically prepared for taking a psychometric test. Research has shown that people perform better in all kinds of psychometric tests when they are well rested and in good physical shape. And, strangely, people do better in tests when they are slightly hungry, so eat lightly before taking one!

Don't judge yourself by what other people say after the test. There's bound to be some know-it-all who claims to have answered everything right in half the time. Even if you're certain you've done badly, don't worry—the test is not the only thing you're being assessed on. There are plenty of opportunities to let your stunning skills shine through.

FIVE TEST-TAKING TIPS

1   Practise using example tests on the internet beforehand.
2   Check the answers. If you get any wrong, find out why.
3   Do the practice test again and again until you get all the answers right.

4   Don't get stressed if you don't finish these tests. They are
    designed so that people rarely actually finish.
5   For personality tests, don't try to pre-empt what sort of
    personality they are looking for—it's no use trying to portray
    something that you are not.

WHERE NEXT?

doctorjob testing zone: **doctorjob.com/TestingZone**
Note that some sites do charge for more in-depth personal testing
and feedback, or may ask you to sign up to their mailing list.

Test your . . . aptitude
SHL Direct: **www.shldirect.com**
PSL: **www.psl.co.uk**
The Morrisby Organisation: **www.morrisby.co.uk**
ASE: **www.ase-solutions.co.uk/support.asp?id=62**
Queendom: **www.queendom.com**

Test your . . . personality
Know Your Type (A Myers-Briggs type indicator test, which costs
around $100): **www.knowyourtype.com**
Hale Online (similar to the above, but only 99 cents):
www.haleonline.com/psychtest
Mental muscle diagram indicator: **www.teamtechnology.co.uk**
The Keirsey Temperament Sorter: **www.keirsey.com**
The IPIP-NEO: **www.personalitytest.net/ipip/ipipneo300.htm**
Out of service: **www.outofservice.com**
PeopleMaps: **www.peoplemaps.co.uk**
Queendom: **www.queendom.com**
Tickle: **uk.tickle.com**

JUGGLING JOB OFFERS

GETTING STARTED

It's a nice problem, if there is such a thing. You receive a job offer from company B, when you've got an interview coming up with first-choice company A and an assessment centre for your dream job with company A++. So what do you do?

Option 1: a bird in the hand . . .

. . . is worth two in the bush. You could take the view that times are tough for graduates and that you should be grateful for any offers you get. It's not unreasonable. After all, you quite liked company B—more than you thought you would. And the people you met at company A weren't *that* nice. Just take the job offer and be mellow.

Option 2: the grass is greener on the other side . . .

You're the kind of person who doesn't like to compromise. You know what you want and you go out and get it. The word 'failure' isn't in your dictionary. Clichés like that are all very well until that too-thin white envelope arrives on your doorstep. And by then, unfortunately, it'll be too late to withdraw the polite letter turning down your offer from company B. But what the hell, take the risk and enjoy the thrill of gambling.

Option 3: buy some time

Options one and two are clearly rubbish. You'll probably always regret the former, and the latter stands a reasonable chance of going horribly wrong. To make a comparison, most people's love lives consist of finding a compromise between waiting for Mr Right to come along and marrying the first bloke who asks you out. And so it is with jobs.

If company B's offer is accompanied by a deadline, then it could be worth trying to get it extended. This means a bit of diplomacy and negotiation, but it could be worth it. You'll probably need to ring the person who offered you the position and talk through the situation, with tact and a modicum of honesty. Explain that you have further interviews coming up and that, rather than rushing into it, you'd like to make the decision to accept with all the facts at your disposal. If you play your cards right, you'll make it sound like company B is really your first choice, but you'd like to set your mind at rest by at least completing the interview process you've started with the others (probably best not to name them, unless you're asked directly).

Of course, they could just say 'no'. A deadline's a deadline and all that. In which case you're back to square one, (but maybe with a little more knowledge about how company B deals with people). And you certainly shouldn't be any worse off than before you made the phone call.

Option 666: accept the offer—then withdraw it

If option three is so clearly right, why have you got this niggling desire to go for the evil solution? Well, we've all got our devilish side, so here are a few thoughts . . .

✔ A written acceptance of the job could put you in breach of
   contract if you then withdraw it. It's unlikely that anyone's going
   to sue a penniless graduate for this, but it's best to be safe.
✔ You never know when you might encounter company B again.
   They could be potential clients or a possible source of work in the
   future (when you're made redundant from company A?) They will
   without doubt have recorded your details in an internal database,
   ready to retrieve when they next encounter you.
✔ Such databases are increasingly widely used. As far as we know,
   so far, people are only checked for stuff like credit ratings and
   qualifications. However, who's to say that companies won't share
   all kinds of non-confidential info in the future—including details
   of you going back on your word?

With your halo restored, you're now ready to go for option three—or fall head over heels for company B. At least that's a genuine choice.

IF IT ALL GOES HORRIBLY WRONG, DON'T PANIC

It's possible to do everything right and still not get an interview. It's possible to shine at interview but not be selected for an assessment centre. It's possible to keep getting to the final stage without receiving a job offer. Everything's possible, and luck does have a part to play—but there might be some positive action you could take. Have a think about the following . . .

I'm not getting any interviews
✔ Are you applying for the right jobs? Be honest.
✔ Have you shown your application form or CV to someone else for them to check?
✔ Have you talked things through with a careers advisor?

I'm not getting any further than first interviews
✔ Do you feel confident immediately after the interview?
✔ Have you prepared well and were your answers deep enough?

While the memory is fresh, write down exactly what you think went wrong. It may be that you're giving off the wrong signals—organise a practice interview with a careers adviser.

I keep failing assessment centres
✔ Is there a particular part of the process that you find difficult?
✔ Are you happy with your performance?
✔ Have you asked for feedback?

Work on areas you find difficult—tests and presentations are often a problem and you can practise both. Fid out whether the careers service is running practice assessment centres. Act on feedback and stay positive. It's only a matter of time . . .

NEGOTIATING A BETTER PACKAGE FOR YOUR NEW JOB

GETTING STARTED

If you make it through the tests and convince your interviewers of your fantastic worth, a job offer may be just around the corner and you face having to talk about the nitty-gritty: your financial value.

Although many graduate training schemes have set starting salaries, there are loads of other jobs where you'll need to exercise your negotiation skills. When you are offered a job, you have a unique opportunity to position yourself as a valuable asset in the organisation and to set your level of remuneration accordingly. To achieve this, you need to establish an appropriate asking price—and it is wise to think about this early in case it should come up during your interview. On the one hand, you don't want to oversell yourself and price yourself out of the market. On the other hand, you need to avoid selling yourself short, as it's extremely difficult to change your position significantly once you've been placed in a complex pay structure. Some people have spent the first few years in a new job trying to make up the gap between their salary and colleagues in the same role.

There are no hard and fast rules about how or when to conduct your negotiation. Every situation is different and each employer will have their own set of thresholds. Understanding the context in which your negotiation is going to take place and being sensitive to the culture of the organisation is therefore essential. Having said that, there are some practical steps you can take to position yourself sensibly.

RESEARCH THE EMPLOYER

When you are going for a job, you are effectively a salesperson promoting a product, and it is up to you to demonstrate that the 'product' is valuable, high-quality and superior to anything a competitor could offer.

Potential employers, or 'buyers', are looking for the best value for their money, so will be driving the deal in the opposite direction. However, if you have positioned yourself well and made a good impression at interview, they won't want to risk losing you and will be prepared to settle at the top of the market rather than at the bottom. If you know what the employer can afford, you will automatically gain an advantage.

Research before entering the negotiation. Familiarise yourself with the company itself, as well as the range of salary and benefit options on offer.

FIVE TIPS FOR RESEARCHING YOUR SALARY

1   Look at the range of packages offered for similar positions in the adverts online or on the jobs pages.
2   Ask for advice from people in your professional and personal network.
3   Ask a contact in the industry to advise you—or use his or her own network to access the information.
4   Approach your local Training and Enterprise Council.
5   If you are a member of a union, they will have information on acceptable salary ranges for your profession.

You can put off a prospective employer by pitching too high *or* too low, so it is important to get your level right. Get a feel for the market rate by drawing information from the above sources. You will also find listings on the internet that can help you; some of these are listed at the end of this chapter.

DISCUSS SALARY AS LATE AS POSSIBLE

It's best to leave salary discussions until the point at which you are offered the job. However, it is not always the case that this will be left until the final stages of the process.

Many recruiters ask for salary expectations and details of current salary early in the process. Some even screen people out on this basis. If this is the case, you may need to spend some time researching the question of salary at the application stage or before the first meeting. This will require you to think about your aspirations and to be absolutely sure of the territory you would like to tread, the experience you would like to gain and the context in which you would like to work.

If you are forced to answer a question about your salary hopes at the beginning of the recruitment process, have a figure ready that is at the higher end of the scale. You can always supplement this with a request for a particular benefits package.

> If the salary offered is less than you had hoped for, you can discuss the benefits package and make provision for an early salary review. If you have a job already, don't assume you'll be offered more than your former salary—especially if you're competing with someone who is equally qualified but willing to work for less.

CONSIDER THE WHOLE PACKAGE

Make sure you check out the salary package, not just the number of zeroes on your payslip. The extra things an employer offers may be worth more than their weight in gold, but they might just be thrown in to make the company seem more appealing.

Some employers have fixed-scale salaries, in which case there is little room for negotiation. However, you may find that the total package of pay and benefits raises the worth of the salary to an acceptable level. For instance, you may be offered private health cover, a non-contributory pension, a fully-financed car and/or significant bonus potential.

You may be able to negotiate a cash equivalent in place of a benefit, particularly in a smaller organisation that is more flexible.

When bonuses are mentioned you may want to discuss the basis on which the bonus is paid so that you are absolutely clear of the terms and conditions attached to it. Some bonus schemes spread the payments over several years as an incentive to stay with the business. Such complexities can be very offputting.

Remember the tax implications. All the benefits included in a package are taxed as 'benefits in kind'. For example, read the note on company cars and health insurance below.

Salary, benefits and incentives: a jargon buster

Bonus. It's pretty obvious . . . bonuses are extra payments. They're often related to the company's performance, but some are awarded for individual excellence. Many companies give a Christmas bonus, which can be useful for buying presents or if you want to soak up some winter sunshine.

Commission. If you work in sales or marketing, you may get commission. You have a basic salary, and for every sale you make, you get a percentage of the profit. The more you sell, the more you earn. You have more motivation, which is good for you and for the company.

Company car. A free car from your new employer? Sounds fantastic . . . what's the catch? Bear in mind that there are financial implications; company cars are taxed on the basis of the price when first registered. You may want to consider whether you need a car with a large capacity, or whether running a car with a smaller engine could improve your income tax situation. As a result of the rapid depreciation of new cars, many people are now opting for a salary increase instead of a car allowance. If you've already got a car, you may get an allowance, paid with your salary, instead. This may be more economical if you don't plan to drive much. If you do want to take the company car, find out whether you or the company will be paying for the petrol, and if you get any personal mileage.

Golden hello. A golden hello is a special bonus awarded when you join a company. You could use the money to buy new clothes for your new job, as a deposit on a house or a flat, or for a season ticket. Employers realise that moving and starting a new job can be expensive, so a golden hello is designed to help you settle into your new position.

Health insurance. Private health insurance, in essence, means you'll be able to have consultations, tests and operations without joining the end of an NHS waiting list. It's just like any other health insurance, but you don't have to pay for it. In some cases the insurance will cover your immediate family as well. Again, bear in mind that you will have to pay income tax on the cash value of the health insurance.

Mobile phone. You know what a mobile phone is. Some companies provide you with one for calls connected to work. This is particularly useful if your job entails lots of time out of the office. Some phones are exclusively for work-related calls, but your employer may cover some personal calls as well.

Pension plan. It seems ridiculous to start saving for your old age when you're starting your first job, but it's not. Really. Large companies often have their own schemes; others have recommended providers. Usually you put in a little money each month, your company puts some in too, and the taxman returns some of what he took. By the time you reach retirement, you'll have a nice pot of money.

When negotiating, be persuasive and consistent in your arguments but be prepared to compromise.

EXPLORE THE BOUNDARIES

Adverts sometimes carry salary ranges to give applicants an idea of the boundaries of the negotiation. You can be sure, however, that the negotiation will start at base level.

If you find that the employer is not responding to your sales pitch, you could negotiate an early pay review instead: for instance, if you demonstrate your worth against certain criteria in the first six months of employment, they will agree to a particular salary increase. Ensure that the criteria are clearly set, though, and that they are included in your contract of employment.

Some adverts state that the salary is 'negotiable'. The onus is then on you to move in with an offer. Again, try and leave it to the end of the recruitment process, and be sure that you have studied the equivalent packages for the type of role and industry sector you are applying for.

If you are successful in your negotiations, ask for the agreed terms and conditions confirmed in writing ASAP.

When negotiating for a package, try to do it calmly and assertively. Appearing too eager can defeat your negotiation. Being too laid back or diffident can portray a lack of professionalism or overconfidence. Either approach can damage your case.

THREE COMMON MISTAKES IN SALARY NEGOTIATIONS

1 **Not doing your research.** It is a common, misguided belief that requesting a high salary will convey a greater sense of your worth. The prospective employer will naturally ask why you think you are worth so much. If you don't have a rational argument, you will look ill-prepared and unprofessional. Time invested in research is always well spent. In this way, you can argue your case logically and professionally.

2 **Bluffing.** Don't bluff in your negotiation and try to play off fictitious job offers against the real one you're hoping to get. Employers generally don't respond to this kind of pressure, and instead of receiving a speedy offer you're likely to be left with nothing. However, if you do genuinely have another offer be candid about what you are being offered (without giving away the other organisation's name)

3 **Being too interested in the package.** Beware of seeming more interested in the package than in the role you are being recruited for. Every employer knows that you will want a fair deal, but you need to demonstrate that your financial concerns are balanced by a genuine desire for the job.

YOUR
FIRST DAY
. . . AND
BEYOND

21

GETTING USED TO
WORKING LIFE

GETTING STARTED

Getting up early, commuting, pension schemes, expenses forms, not being able to get blasted on a Tuesday night, struggling with office equipment, office politics, office parties . . . the trouble with working life is that it's fiendishly complicated.

So, you've landed your dream job and you're now entering uncharted territory. Remember, your first few days are extremely important in making the right impression and can have a lasting effect. Here are some guidelines to help ease the transition from student to working life.

- ✔ Go shopping! A working professional needs a working wardrobe. Think about what people were wearing when you went for your interview and try to fit in with this.
- ✔ Reread any information you already have about your new employers. You could even phone your new boss to ask for any additional material that might help you.
- ✔ Be friendly and approachable and attempt to build the foundations of a good relationship with your work colleagues.
- ✔ Make sure you know what is expected of you. If you are worried about any particular aspects of your work, talk things over with your boss.
- ✔ If you are set deadlines make sure that you meet them.

✔ Try to get an understanding of the organisational structure, the relationship of your job to others and the preferred communication networks (phone, face-to-face, memos, e-mail etc).

Networking

Networking, dahling, is a key part of your career progression. The working world is as interested in *who* you know as in *what* you know. Never has this been so true as in today's fluid job market. Once you've secured your first position the idea is to use your interaction with other professionals as an opportunity to network and tap into influential resources for building your career. It's rumoured that 85 percent of all job vacancies in the USA are unadvertised—and what happens over the pond today always arrives here sooner or later.

Networking is a skill that can be learnt like any other. Just keep in mind that this doesn't just have to be a means to an end (the end being your personal advancement), it's also a great way to make new friends and widen your social circle. Personal advancement, like networking, is itself a bit of a nebulous concept anyway. It doesn't necessarily mean new jobs or even promotion. It's about working on interesting projects, storing up experience and even building up an address book of potential clients should you ever go freelance.

Be patient: by its very nature networking is a long-term strategy.

Office parties

The office party is a breeding ground for gossip and humiliation. It's also your annual chance to tell the managing director that you could run the company better, to inform your manager that you deserve a pay rise and to declare your undying love for the receptionist. It's the time you catch all sorts of people getting up to all sorts of mischief. You may even stumble across the boss in a compromising position with one of your colleagues. Whilst at the time you may plan how to use this information to your advantage, you should resist the temptation of blackmail once you're sober.

To avoid throwing up in public or falling unconscious in the toilets, the general advice is to keep circulating and try not to drink too much—although, granted, this may be a tad difficult if the booze is free. You should, in an ideal world, leave at the first sign of trouble involving your inebriated self.

For members of either sex, don't get too carried away with provocative attire. Libidos tend to be a bit feverish at these events. By all means set pulses racing, but you don't want to be seen as the office tramp. And remember that friendliness can be misconstrued if accompanied with physical contact—particularly of the lip-to-lip kind. But if an office party snog does become an office party one-night stand, follow these obvious and very sensible guidelines: use protection and be discreet. You should also agree on a 'morning after' game plan. 'Thanks for a good night' shows you can be adult about the situation, but if you spill the juicy details with colleagues be prepared for him/her to do the same.

There are some useful lessons for us all at:
www.angelfire.com/ny3/slimsin/work.html

Business cards

Flash it, flaunt it, love it! The business card is the professional working person's new best friend and should be handed around at every opportunity. Those who don't have them may see the parading of business cards as showing off, but they're only jealous.

At this stage in your career, you may only have given them to your friends and family, but you'll soon find them an important means of networking and making valuable contacts. It ensures that people don't forget your name. So, don't leave them in a drawer or in a pile on your desk. Take advantage of these pocket-sized status symbols to establish yourself in the business world and interact with professionals using a language they understand and respond to.

Expenses

Ah, the bliss of working. If you're lucky, you can get 'em to pay for anything. Extended lunches, evening meals, boozy dos with a 'client', long distance phone calls . . . If you're going to work all the hours your employer demands of you, you might as well get something back for your efforts.

And strangely, you'll find that most big-company cultures heartily endorse this attitude. Really. If you're away from the office for any period of time, you could be staying in swanky hotels with a fifty-quid-a-night budget for booze and thrills. Well, perhaps not. But you might be surprised at the generosity of some companies. They will look after you, to the extent that it feels strange when you have to pay for the drinks yourself.

On the other hand, there are small companies where every penny spent is counted in the gritty hope that the pounds will look after themselves. While your management consultant friends moan that every Hilton looks the same, you'll be struggling with a four-pounds-a-head lunch budget and a no-taxis rule. Even in quite reasonable companies there will be issues, like how much petrol money your boss is willing to pay. The standard is about 40p a mile at the moment, but with petrol prices these days it might be wise to keep an eye on this. Don't be tempted by ingenious petrol scams, though. You have to play expenses by the rules. The consequences of getting found out are far more significant than the amounts to be made.

So however large the largesse of your employer, it's worth finding out what you're entitled to. At the very worst, it might save you from a verbal warning. And at best you could find you're one of the lucky ones who gets a company credit card early on in your career. One can only cringe with jealousy at the temptation this might provide . . .

AND FINALLY . . . PARENTS

Who they? You know—those old people who fed and watered you for two decades.

Be prepared for yet another stage in the cycle of your relationship with your parents. The days when you were bored of their company two hours into the Easter holiday will soon be long gone. Once you've moved out and have real adult responsibilities and the pressure of a grown-up job, you may actually look forward to seeing them again.

You're likely to start seeing your parents as people, rather than as bank accounts on legs. You might even enjoy their company now that you're no longer bleeding them dry. Occasions like Christmas and Easter will assume greater importance as family reunions rather than a free piss-up. It'll take a little while to adjust to your new independence, but it's reassuring to know that they're just a phone call away, and are always useful for free accommodation when you want to go back to the nest for a while.

Finally, while your parents may have some valid advice for you as you set out on your new life (particularly if you're going into the same field as one of them, or into the family business), things have moved on since their day. Employers no longer necessarily look for the same things as when your parents started job hunting, and their perception of the new-graduate workplace is probably at least 20 years out of date. They may want you to achieve their unfulfilled ambitions, or have a distorted view of what they think you want to achieve; for all they know you may still want to be a ballerina or a fireman. So listen by all means, but don't let them pressure you into something you're unsure about. You've been practising independent life for at least 3 years; it's now time to put it into practice.

MANAGING YOUR TIME

GET ORGANISED

We've all seen job ads asking for time-management skills, but what do these skills actually mean when transferred to the workplace? In our working lives, time is the one thing that is in ever-increasing demand.

Time management is about making every moment effective by being truly focused and not dividing your energies by worrying about the past or the future. However, it's still important to be able to keep the past, present and future in perspective so that you can plan and prioritise effectively, gaining a sense of order, structure and security. To make sure employees use their time effectively and don't idly while away the hours exploring the web and sending personal e-mails, employers will train you and even ask you to fill in timesheets. But even this doesn't guarantee good time management.

In layman's terms, time management is all about prioritising tasks, avoiding and controlling distractions, increasing efficiency and reducing stress. The result, in an ideal world, should be increased productivity and a better work-life balance. You will be more in control of your workload and can avoid staying late at work or taking work home with you. What it's not about is staring vacantly at your computer screen while musing over what's for dinner or planning your evening's telly viewing.

Good time management allows a certain amount of time every day for the usual distractions, interruptions, crises and stuff-that-goes-horribly-wrong. If that all sounds terribly alien, think back to how you got through your degree. At the very least, you must have learnt how *not* to manage your time.

Be aware of your choices

The desire to improve your time management skills is half the battle, but you need to be aware of the choices you have to make. These relate to your overall life balance and the values you hold.

Look at what you're being asked to do at work and why. Is this because it's related to your role or because you hold a particular skill or expertise? If you're being asked to do many things outside your area of responsibility, you may need to speak to your boss to clarify your job boundaries .

> **Being able to prioritise will save you hours. If you're managing someone, you may find that you can delegate some tasks to a member of your team. Remember to give clear instructions and a deadline.**

There are always choices to be made. You may find that you can win more time by working from home, thus avoiding time spent on commuting. However, in doing this you will need to create boundaries to ensure that your productivity remains high and that domestic trivia isn't allowed to intrude.

Plan for lost time

Lost time accumulated over a period has a surprisingly large impact on the time available for other activities. You get a build-up of 'negative time'. If you can, plan pockets of space in your day to accommodate unforeseen extra jobs, meetings running over etc. This releases pressure and allows you to get back on track.

Be prepared to change behavioural habits

Be aware of any patterns that characterise the way you manage your time. You may find that you're constantly overrunning in meetings or that you pick up a lot of extra work because you aren't assertive enough in saying 'no'. All these factors consume time that you may not have available.

> **Be honest about how long things take. Don't try to do the impossible or get hung up on process.**

Prioritise and plan ahead

Look at your workload and categorise your tasks into those that are important to your overall role, those which will add benefit to your role but may not be central, and those things that you do that you may be good at but which are outside your area of responsibility.

Set yourself definite and specific goals. What do you want to achieve in the time that you have? It is best to write these goals down. Make sure that they are achievable and set yourself a realistic deadline. It may help to divide the task up so that you can take it step by step. This will make the completing of the task more rewarding, as you can measure your progress on the way.

We often get caught up in responding to others' expectations and sacrificing our own choices. As you undertake your time audit, make sure that you're not spending time on unnecessary activities that don't serve your purpose. Delegate wherever you can, but don't expect others to do what you can't do or to pick up the mess you leave.

> **It's important to remember that your view of what is a priority may be different from someone else's; take time to talk to all the relevant people to make sure that misunderstandings don't occur.**

Planning is essential. It will help you to prioritise, anticipate problems and potential conflicts, and see where you are going. Be aware of time pressures as you plan.

TIME MANAGEMENT TOOLKITS

There are a number of time management tools that help people to order their days—but they're only as useful as the time invested in using them. These include:

✔ 'to do' lists
✔ categorising work according to its level of importance and focusing only on the essential
✔ aligning tasks to business goals and objectives and cutting out the 'nice to do'
✔ shared diaries (e.g. team, secretarial, professional groups)
✔ BlackBerries and Palm Pilots

It's not easy to make the transition from depending on a diary and Post-It notes to organising your life with a BlackBerry, so allow for time to get used to the device and to transfer your information. You could use a dual system for a few weeks, then throw the paper diary away.

In moments of desperation, people often rush out and buy the latest time-management technology, which can be both expensive and complicated. It's always worth considering what is motivating you to make that purchase. No system can compensate entirely for your own inadequacies; it can only help you to deal with them. It is much better to take time to get to the root of the problem and see what the cause is. Once this has been established, you can identify the best approach to time management for you.

Don't expect too much of yourself

Remember that a new environment takes some getting used to. When we try to change too many things at once, pressure is bound to cause us to step back into old habits. While the logic in time management appears straightforward, the complexity of our lives means that managing time is not straightforward. The key is to take small steps, heading towards clear goals.

How we manage our time can become habitual. We all know people who are always late or people who are always early. The way you plan your life and time rapidly takes on a pattern. Breaking that pattern can mean that we have to change the way we view ourselves and the world in which we live, and we may need to ask for support from others in making that change. Don't be afraid to ask friends, family and trusted colleagues for their help.

AVOIDING INFORMATION OVERLOAD

With the rise of e-mail, the internet and technology in general, the amount of information available to us is rapidly increasing. As a result, we are all expected to absorb and respond to more information than ever before.

The problem is that we have to deal with this influx without any preparation, training or time! Often, we find it difficult to process the flood of information—we feel as though we're drowning, struggling to find time for more important tasks. The good news is that there are steps you can take to keep your head above water.

SIX TIPS FOR STAYING IN CONTROL

1   Identify any time-wasting e-mails and attachments and delete them.
2   Ask to be removed from the list of often unnecessary 'everyone' e-mails.
3   Request a good spam filter from the IT department.
4   Prioritise your e-mails and delete those that are low priority
5   Return calls only to those people you need to speak to
6   Look at a piece of data only once before deciding what to do with it. If you miss something important, you can be sure that it will come back to you.

Seek information efficiently

When you are researching something, aim for the 'Pareto Principle'. This holds that 20% of what you access probably holds 80% of the information you need. Anxiety causes people to spend excessive time wading through every piece of data available. It's technology that allows this to happen. People used to make decisions in ambiguous situations; it was considered to be a management skill. Develop your instincts along with your knowledge.

Surfing the Web is incredibly seductive, with each link taking you further and further into fascinating but unnecessary detail. Decide how much time you'll spend in each session, print the information that is relevant and leave the rest in the ether.

Find your own preferred places for accessing information and discipline yourself to go there only. Look only at data that is relevant to your job, the project you're working on or the decision you're making. Resist the temptation to be intrigued by those things that lie outside your area of responsibility. Too often, people are sucked into irrelevant detail because they don't know where to draw the line.

As we all know, the internet is freely available—which is its advantage and its disadvantage. Anyone can set up a website, whatever the quality, and you can spend hours looking for the high-quality information you need. Being very specific in your searches will reduce the time that you spend looking for the information you want, as will adding the most productive sites to your list of favourites. You could also set time limits on your Web searches, knowing that you will probably pick up most of the information you need in the first ten minutes or so.

When you find a really useful website, bookmark it and use it as your first port of call.

Learn to say 'no'

Try not to be the dumping ground for information that others don't want to wade through. Many will try to pass the burden on to you if you even hint at being receptive to the task. Take control of what lands in your inbox and decide not to be held to ransom by a piece of data.

Limit your availability. Switch your mobile off for periods during the day when you need to concentrate, or let your voicemail field calls for you. This way you can determine who to speak to and when to schedule the conversations. Anyone who needs to speak to you urgently will find a way of getting through to you.

Regulate information

Learn to throw things away. Have the courage to throw data away or delete files when you have exhausted their usefulness. You can always access the same data again—and when you do, it will probably have been updated.

Watch that you don't get bogged down in detail. People often fear they'll miss an essential piece of information if they don't comb through every available source. In fact this rarely happens. Resist the temptation to scrutinise every piece of information that appears on your screen or arrives on your desk.

Not being able to switch off from the need to absorb or generate information can be tiring and stressful. Blood pressure can rise, mental faculties can deteriorate, and any patience you may have had can disappear altogether. Just as the body needs time to relax, so does the mind—and not just when you're sleeping. Quieting the mind through techniques such as meditation or yoga has been proven to increase health, improve memory and stimulate creativity. It has also been linked to increased productivity and a sense of wellbeing. If these techniques don't appeal, try listening to music, reading or taking gentle exercise. Anything that allows the mind to 'freewheel' will prove beneficial.

> **WHERE NEXT?**
>
> BlackBerry: **www.blackberry.com**
> Mindtools: **www.mindtools.com/pages/main/newMN_HTE.htm**
> Palm: **www.palm.com/uk**
> Time Management Guide: **www.manage-your-time.com**
> Total Success (time management training programmes):
> **www.tsuccess.dircon.co.uk/timemanagementtips.htm**

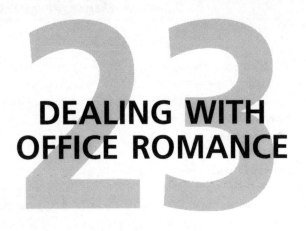

DEALING WITH OFFICE ROMANCE

LOVE IS IN THE AIR . . .

As we spend so much time at work, it's no surprise that many people have romantic relationships with colleagues.

Many people who had an office romance have regretted it, for one reason or another. A lot of office politics is based on jealousy, with people feeling 'slighted' for either real or imaginary reasons; so, if you work in an environment where office politics are rife, office romances (or the gossip surrounding them) can get out of hand. This chapter offers advice for anyone involved in, or affected by, an office romance.

60% More than 60% of people have had a relationship with a work colleague. More than half of these said it had affected their work. Source: survey quoted in the *Guardian*, January 2004

THE PROS AND CONS

People find romance in the office for many reasons.

Most full-time employees spend over 35 hours a week at work, so they necessarily build friendships with others there. Conversations can spring up in the canteen or by the photocopier or kettle. If you work in a very specialised industry, work might be the one place that you can find people who share some of your interests.

It's easy to get carried away in the first flush of attraction for someone, but, if you work with that person too, think about the following:

✔ Does the company you work for actively rule out dating at work?
✔ Is the other person your boss, or are you theirs?
✔ How would you deal with office gossip if you became a couple?
✔ Will there be accusations of favouritism?
✔ Will you still be able to do your job properly?
✔ How would you cope if the relationship ended badly?

Dating a peer

Going out with someone who has the same level of responsibilities as you, if not exactly the same job, might look like the safest option. If nothing else, spending so much time at work with someone else means that you have a good chance of getting to know them quite well before you become a couple. On the down-side, working with your partner means that you never really get a break from them. You might find that you end up talking about work a lot even when you're not there, and if you have to work together on a project that becomes fraught, friction could be introduced into the relationship.

> Remember that, if you work near your partner (on the same floor or at a neighbouring desk, for example), you may find it hard if other people try to flirt with him or her. This will not only make you unhappy, but will also cause your work to suffer.

If your partner does have the same job as you, things could get tricky if the chance of a promotion comes up. Only one person can get that new post, and if you've both applied, but one of you is the successful applicant, things are bound to be tense.

Remember that, in extreme cases, people who were once in a relationship find it impossible to work with each other once it's over. Some people even go to the lengths of changing their core working hours so that they can avoid their ex-partner. Others may decide to leave the company completely.

Dating your boss or a senior member of staff

Whispers of favouritism may start to build if you start a relationship with someone higher up the career ladder than you. If your partner is your manager, you're putting yourself in a potentially difficult situation, regardless of whether things go well or badly. If you get a promotion, some people are bound to think (and to say out loud) that you didn't win it on your own merits, but just because of your relationship. If your relationship ends and your career takes a nose-dive at the same time, you may feel that events in your private life are affecting your professional life and that you're being treated unfairly.

Dating someone more junior than you

If you are your partner's manager, things are much more complicated. Even if you break the news to other people before they find out for themselves, some people are much more likely to think that your partner will be getting preferential treatment in terms of responsibilities, pay and promotion prospects, for example.

Even if you make a concerted effort not to treat your partner differently from anyone else, you may find that you do it subconsciously in one of two ways: either you *will* be easier on your partner than you are with other team members, or you'll try to counteract accusations of favouritism by being harder on your partner than you need to be. You also need to think about how you'd deal with situations that may crop up in a downturn. You may have to make your partner redundant, for example. Would your relationship be able to survive that?

As with any office romance, if things don't go as well as you'd expected and you break up, the aftermath can be difficult. The atmosphere may be terrible, and he or she may refuse to work with you and ask to be transferred to another team.

Dating a key supplier, external partner, or competitor

Sometimes, romances can occur between people who don't work for the same company, but for two companies that work very closely together. For example, one person may work for a printer and the other person for a paper supplier. While you may not see your partner all day every day at work, you may still run the risk of damaging your company's interests if it were to end badly.

FIND OUT IF YOUR COMPANY HAS A POLICY ON THIS ISSUE

Some businesses do see office romances as something other than inno-cent flirtation that makes the day go by more quickly.

For example, they may worry that such romances could:

✔ encourage conflict amongst colleagues (if someone feels jealous of another person, for example)
✔ reduce productivity (if the couple spend a good part of their working day talking to, e-mailing or phoning each other about non-work issues)
✔ compromise decision making
✔ allow competitors to gain an unfair advantage

Businesses tend to tackle the issue of office romances in one of three ways:

1 they ignore them.
2 they are opposed to them. In the United States, some companies have 'no-dating' policies, which are intended to prevent problems arising from employee relationships in the workplace (such as preferential treatment or claims of sexual harassment if a relation-ship breaks down). The policies define what constitutes acceptable and unacceptable behaviour and what action will be taken if the terms of the policy are violated. No-dating policies are still a

relatively small-scale way of dealing with romance at work, and concerns have been raised that they may adversely affect employees' right to privacy.

3   they realise that office romances are unavoidable, and set up a formal way of recording them to protect both themselves and the employees. Some businesses have adopted a practice that originated in the United States, where they ask employees to notify their managers if they enter into a relationship at work and to sign an agreement that states that the relationship is consensual. These agreements are sometimes called 'cupid' or 'love' contracts and may be used where an employer requires notification of such relationships, especially between supervisors and their subordinates. The agreement may also stipulate that the relationship will not affect or interfere with the work of those involved.

If you're involved in a long-term relationship with a colleague, check what your company's views are on office romances (someone in human resources should be able to help you). If there's a policy in place, comply fully and tell your manager as soon as you can.

IF YOU DECIDE TO GO AHEAD . . .

Be sure it's what you want

A kiss at the Christmas party is one thing, but a full-blown relationship with a colleague is a different matter. It could affect your job and your prospects radically, so be as sure as you can that it's a good idea for you. If you're new to the company, try to find out discreetly if the other party has a history of going out with people from the office or has a partner at home that he or she is keeping quiet about!

If you feel you're being pressurised into a relationship you don't want, take action immediately. You have a right to go to work without being harassed. Talk to your boss about the situation if you can, but if your boss is the other party, contact someone in human resources or your boss's line manager.

Be discreet

If you are in a relationship at work or are about to embark on one, it's important to be discreet. Don't tell anyone who doesn't need to know, and act appropriately at all times in any work dealings with your partner. If anyone does ask you directly about your relationship, be honest and say 'yes, I am dating X', but there's no need to go any further than that. People will find something and someone else to talk about soon enough.

Think about how to deal with issues such as arriving or leaving the office together. If you work physically close to your partner and your colleagues are unaware of your relationship, they may quickly put two and two together if you start to go home or turn up at the same time. Think about how you want to play this so that you keep the fuss to a minimum but also cut down on the stress you may be feeling at having to keep a big part of your life secret.

Do your job

Remember that even though the office has given you the opportunity to find a partner, you still need to do your job when you get there.

If you have to work closely with your partner, keep all your communications professional. Take special care when you're phoning or e-mailing them, and don't write personal information in e-mails, as many companies monitor them. (You may also accidentally send the e-mail to the wrong person!)

Don't spend a lot of time dropping by your partner's desk unless you really need to—remember that you'll not only be disturbing any colleagues sitting close, but also giving them the opportunity to hear what you're saying. This is the type of thing that can really annoy other people and make a sensitive situation much worse.

If your office romance has gone wrong:

✔ If you signed a 'love contract', tell your manager.

✔ Keep your own counsel. Don't tell anyone who doesn't really need to know.

✔ Even if the other party has behaved badly or unfairly, don't badmouth them to other people who work with them. As with most office gossip, what you say will be turned into something far worse by the time it's been through the rumour mill.

✔ Keep a professional distance. This will be hard at first, but if you have to work with your ex-partner often, be polite and get on with your job even if it's the last thing you might feel like doing.

✔ If your ex-partner behaves badly towards you in the workplace, talk to your manager straightaway. Don't let it escalate. Remain as calm as you can, make a note of what happened when, and whether anyone else witnessed the incident.

If you know someone whose office romance has gone wrong:

✔ Be supportive. Try not to say 'I told you so'. Accept that the relationship happened, is now over, and try to support employees who ask for your help.

✔ Keep some perspective. Of course you should step in if you feel someone has gone too far or if you're directly asked for help, but don't get dragged into the aftermath of a messy break-up unnecessarily.

✔ Don't comment on the rights and wrongs of the situation, make disparaging comments about the other party (even if, deep-down, you think they deserve it) or promise something that you might not be able to deliver. For example, if one of the parties comes to you and demands that he or she be moved to a different department or team, say that you'll investigate and get back to him or her.

If you were involved in the relationship and you are more senior:

✔ Talk to your own manager about how best to handle the fallout. Be completely honest, even though you may feel embarrassed. It's much better that he or she be put in the picture as soon as possible, and it's particularly important to check that procedures are followed properly if you are to avoid sexual harassment claims.

FOUR OFFICE ROMANCE NO-NOS

1   **Telling too many people.** It's exciting when you start a new relationship, and if your romance is taking place at the office it could be brightening up your work day too. If you do have an office romance, however, resist the temptation to tell everyone you know what's happening. Be discreet and don't give the resident gossips or troublemakers the opportunity to make you topic of the day.

2   **Not checking your company's policy.** Even if you think an office romance is harmless, your managers might not agree. It may feel awkward, but it's worth checking with your boss (if he or she is not the other party involved!) or someone from human resources whether your company has a no-dating policy or if it requires you to sign a 'love contract'.

3   **Letting your work suffer.** If you're bored at work and looking for a distraction, an office romance might be just what you're looking for. We never know how long relationships will last, so make sure that you carry on doing your job to the best of your ability so that no-one can question your commitment, whatever is happening in your personal life.

4   **Badmouthing your ex-partner at work.** If your office romance doesn't last, don't tell tales or spread rumours about your now ex-partner to his or her colleagues. Break-ups are often difficult, but try to keep calm and remember that anything you say in haste will either come back to haunt you or be exaggerted by someone else, making the whole situation much worse. If your ex is rude about you, talk to your manager immediately.

UNDERSTANDING DIVERSITY AND EQUAL OPPORTUNITIES

DIVERSITY: THE SPICE OF WORKING LIFE

Everybody knows the stereotypes—the straight-white-male investment banker, the female school ma'am and the dizzy blonde secretary. Industries are working harder than ever to dispel these old myths and improve their success at recruiting minority groups.

In terms of diversity, the future looks bright. Employers now appreciate the advantages of a broad cultural mix that can be drawn on to meet the challenges of global business. While the imbalance has by no means been redressed, industries are slowly changing as employers adjust their image and working environment to open up recruitment opportunities to all.

72% of private sector companies see a direct link between diversity and performance. Source: Cabinet Office research, 'The Business of Diversity'

A mirror of society

In an industry such as the **media**, organisations appreciate that their work-force, like their output, should reflect the context in which they operate. Soaps, for example, have shaped up their act by introducing Asian or black families and a more sensitive approach to gay storylines.

Newspapers are also starting to jump on the diversity bandwagon and have recently formed a working group called the National Newspapers Diversity Forum (NNDF) to encourage ethnic minorities to consider a career in journalism. They are, nevertheless, still looking to recruit the most talented individuals, not simply the candidate who will make them look more diverse.

In the **public sector** the need to effectively represent society as a whole is an obvious reason for workforce diversity. Public sector employers have measures in place, such as flexible working, targeted training for under-represented groups and regular scrutiny of organisational processes to ensure that they aren't discriminatory.

Historically, careers such as **investment banking**, **accountancy** and **law** were associated with a specific type of employee, namely the Oxbridge-educated white male. In recent years this has changed considerably, as employers realise that coming to the global table with a homogenous workforce won't be effective.

Of course it's not only ethnic minority candidates that come under the catch-all term of diversity. Female, male, gay, lesbian or transgender appli-cants are all targeted by the recruitment campaigns of various sectors. In the global fast-moving **consumer goods industry**, where innovation and creativity are key, a diverse workforce ensures that, by drawing on their different social and cultural experiences, employees are in touch with customers and generate a wide variety of ideas.

The **teaching profession**, aware of the value of attracting staff as culturally diverse as the pupils they will teach, has been particularly pro-active in trying to promote teaching as a career among ethnic minority groups at universities, through, for example, publications such as *Network News* or *The Voice*.

GENDER

Why is unequal pay still an issue in many sectors when women make up nearly half of the UK workforce?

As female students gradually overtake males in their performance at school and university, traditionally male-dominated professions such as medicine and law are beginning to admit more female graduates than male, though certain sectors, such as the built environment and IT are particularly lacking in women. There are also many professions where men are in the minority, such as primary school teaching, human resources and nursing.

80% Computer science and engineering and technology higher-education courses are still over 80% male.

Source: Equal Opportunities Commission

The law

It's usually quite easy to determine whether someone has been treated less favourably than someone of the opposite sex would have been in identical circumstances. Such discrimination includes instances of sexual harassment (defined as unwelcome physical, verbal or non-verbal conduct of a sexual nature) or treating a female employee or candidate less favourably than her male counterparts because she is pregnant.

The main grey area, termed 'indirect sexual discrimination', is far more subtle. This is where a condition or practice adversely affects a considerably larger proportion of one sex than the other, and it is not justifiable to apply that condition or practice. For example, a requirement to be under 5' 10" would probably discriminate against men. And a requirement to work full time might unlawfully discriminate against women.

The Equal Pay Act binds all employers to award men and women the same amount for doing the same job or a job of equal value. This also covers bonuses, overtime, holiday pay, sick pay, performance-related pay or occupational pensions.

> The Equal Pay Act can't be used to deal with unequal pay where those being compared are of the same sex, regardless of how unfair or irrational the employer's pay arrangements may be.

You can read up on the law, including the Sex Discrimination Act (SDA) and the Equal Pay Act, on the Web—see **Where next?** at the end of this chapter.

Graduate recruitment

Graduate recruiters generally aim to recruit a certain proportion of men and women in each intake, depending on their constitution and requirements.

15% By the age of 24, female graduates earn 15% less than men. Source: Equal Opportunities Commission

Statistics reveal, however, that the issue of equal pay refuses to go away. It has been shown that male graduates in full-time employment earn more than their female counterparts on average, even when:

✔ they have studied the same subject
✔ they have achieved the same class of degree
✔ they work in the same occupation
✔ they are employed in the same industry.

Graduates are advised to ask pertinent questions about equal pay and company-wide pay reviews when they attend interviews. Women are often unaware that male colleagues in identical roles are earning more, as many employers promote a climate of secrecy where salaries are concerned. It is best to tackle this issue before you decide to join an organisation in order to be sure that they really do have a structure of equality.

DISABILITY

If you qualify as disabled you need to know your rights and also what's happening in recruitment that's likely to affect you.

Legally speaking, a disabled person has an 'impairment that has a substantial and long-term adverse effect on their ability to carry out normal day-to-day activities', including:

✔ Physical impairment caused by an accident or experienced from birth (e.g. blindness, deafness, heart disease, paralysis and severe disfigurement).

✔ Mental impairment, including learning disabilities such as dyslexia and all recognised mental illnesses.

On the surface, employers may seem to have embraced disabled people's employment rights, but concrete evidence of this is a bit harder to come by.

78% of disabled respondents to a recent survey felt that the assumption that disabled people need more support prevents employers recruiting disabled staff.
Source: Scope

Many of the country's leading employers recognise the business advantages of recruiting a more diverse workforce and that disabled employees are a vital part of that. Besides their ability to do the job, disabled people have considerable life experience, creative problem-solving skills and the potential to help businesses connect with different sectors of the population. And if an employer makes an adjustment at work, whether to equipment or working practices, an employee is likely to show a similar level of commitment in return.

The law
The most important piece of legislation for disabled employees is the Disability Discrimination Act (DDA). It covers virtually every aspect of employment, but the bottom line is that the employer has a duty to make 'reasonable adjustments' to premises and working practices to ensure that disabled employees are not at a substantial disadvantage compared to others.

If the disability has a significantly adverse affect on your ability to do the job and it can't be remedied by a change in equipment or alteration of the building, you won't be protected by the law. Moreover, certain jobs are exempt under the Act, such as prison officers, fire fighters, police officers, members of the armed forces, employees who work on board ships, aircraft and hovercraft, employees who work largely or wholly outside Great Britain and voluntary workers

There are also exceptions such as hay fever and poor eyesight which are not considered disabilities.

86% of disabled respondents said that poor physical access in the workplace is a barrier to getting employment. Source: Scope

There is a requirement under the DDA to ensure that arrangements for interviews and assessment centres don't put applicants with disabilities at a disadvantage. You may not have disclosed in your application that you have a disability, but you may want to identify practical needs to ensure that you can access the same opportunities as other applicants.

Graduate recruitment

Disability is one area of graduate recruitment that still needs work. While other diversity issues tend to be dealt with fairly and favourably by employers, it's harder to say that the world of graduate recruitment does everything it should to protect disabled job candidates and trainees. There are fewer disabled graduates than there are other diversity groups but, thanks to a slow but steady stream of initiatives, job opportunities have increased and there is more help about.

AGE

People in Britain are living longer than ever before and having fewer children—as a result, our population is ageing.

The reduction in the number of young people coming into the job market means that it is now essential for employers to realise the benefits of age diversity. But this isn't the only reason that employers are taking age diversity more seriously. Since October 2006, it is illegal for UK employers to discriminate against job applicants on the basis of age. The anti-age discrimination laws are similar to those for disability, gender, ethnicity and sexual orientation, and businesses that fail to comply with them will face prosecution.

According to The Employers Forum on Age (EFA), age discrimination in the workplace exists when decisions on recruitment, training and promotion are based on a person's age rather than on his or her skills and ability to do a job. This could be an employee who is over 50 and is therefore considered too old to retrain or a 24-year-old employee who is considered too young for a post despite having sufficient experience. Contrary to popular belief, ageism is widespread and affects all age groups.

Graduate recruitment

How, you may wonder, can age can affect graduate recruitment? Graduate schemes will probably be allowed to continue as an acceptable way of recruiting suitably-qualified people; most likely to be affected are those with a maximum age limit. The main objective of the legislation is to put an end to age discrimination at both ends of the scale, ensuring that applicants are recruited on merit and nothing else.

One group who should see the positive effects of change is mature students. Traditionally, if you are older it can be harder to break into your chosen industry. Eligibility for graduate recruitment schemes is a grey area, but under the new legislation, employers can no longer advertise for a mature person over a certain age or specify that they are looking for young gradu-ates to fill a position. So whether you graduate at the age of 25 or 55, your age should no longer be a consideration for your future employer.

RACE, RELIGION AND ETHNICITY

Racial discrimination in the workplace—a crime in any language.

Although law relating to religious discrimination was not introduced in Britain until 2003, race discrimination has been outlawed since 1976. But employers should not be relying on legal requirements. There is no question that discrimination in employment on the grounds of colour, race, ethnic or national origin is wrong. Apart from being unfair to individuals who are denied jobs and access to vocational training, many businesses realise that it is detrimental to their own interests to deny themselves access to the widest possible pool of talent available.

The law

Discrimination on the grounds of race became unlawful with the introduction of the Race Relations Act (RRA) 1976. This Act, together with RRA 1976 (Amendment) Regulations 2003, makes it illegal to discriminate against someone on the grounds of nationality, colour, ethnic or racial group. The RRA makes it unlawful to discriminate in:

✔ recruitment
✔ pay
✔ other terms and conditions (e.g. holidays)
✔ access to opportunities or benefits (e.g. promotion, training, bonuses)
✔ dismissal
✔ disadvantaging a worker in any other way on racial grounds.

There are two types of discrimination forbidden by law: direct discrimination when a worker is treated less favourably on the grounds of race, colour, nationality or ethnicity; and indirect discrimination, which concerns the conditions of application for a particular job, specifically if the conditions cannot be justified by the requirements of the job.

Discrimination on the grounds of religion and belief became unlawful in 2003. In employment, this also covers employment practices such as dress codes. The law isn't just confined to the major faiths though—it considers any religions and faiths that can show collective worship and a clear belief system, and includes lesser-known religions such as Paganism.

The law does have exceptions however. An employer can advertise for a person of a particular race or ethnic origin if there is a genuine occupational requirement for this. For example, a charity specifically for Black communities could say they are interested in hearing from Black applicants, provided they match the job specifications in terms of education and experience.

Graduate recruitment

While there is still much work to be done, many organisations are reviewing with some success their selection practices to recruit more ethnic minority graduates. Things have changed considerably as organisations try to develop understanding of other religions within the workplace to ensure harmony and a celebration of diversity among employees. Many larger organisations also have specific networks and support groups in place for workers from different backgrounds. These groups meet up regularly to discuss religious or cultural issues, such as raising awareness of different faiths within the workplace, and to discuss any related problems—for example, disagreements arising from different beliefs—and any requests for leave during religious festivals. Some employers even create a place for prayer and for workers who may want or need to take some time out of the office.

SEXUAL ORIENTATION

While we're happy to report that graduate recruiters generally don't seem to be guilty of discrimination on the basis of sexual orientation, you still need to know your rights.

With the new Civil Partnership Act coming into effect in 2005 and recent anti-discrimination legislation, lesbian, gay and bisexual (LGB) rights are official in the workplace. Harassment and discrimination haven't magically disappeared—it's just that the law will offer more help than before. Employers seem increasingly committed to LGB rights, and there is an increasing number of equal opportunities statements and LGB employee networks and associations.

So how can you target gay-friendly employers? Well, as with most job hunting, it's all a matter of research. Although many employers are gay-friendly, you might want to look particularly at those who make a particular effort to recruit you. Newspapers and magazines serving the lesbian, gay and bisexual communities often publish job advertisements; these are a good indication that an employer is actively gay-friendly—as is any involvement with equal opportunities initiatives on your campus or in your town.

Check with the campaign group Stonewall to see if the organisation participates in the Diversity Champions programme or has a diversity officer.

On the question of revealing your sexuality on applications or at interview—remember it entirely depends on what you feel comfortable with. Discuss any worries with your family or friends and make sure you know the law and your rights.

24% of lesbians, gay men or bisexuals have avoided certain jobs, careers or employers for fear of discrimination because of their sexuality. Source: Stonewall

The law
Although discrimination does still linger, victims of discrimination can now sue for damages, provided they can show that they have been treated differently because they are gay, lesbian or bisexual.

Under the Civil Partnership Act, equal pensions and benefits must now be provided to same-sex partners as to married (i.e. heterosexual) couples. The new law won't just change things for couples who have legally committed to each other: it means that same-sex couples in general will have the same rights (often dependent upon whether a couple is cohabiting or sharing finances) as unmarried heterosexual couples.

44% of lesbian, gay or bisexual trade unionists reported that they had suffered discrimination because of their sexuality. Source: TUC

If you're worried about anything, talk to your human resources department and get them to clarify their equal opportunity policies, which could include benefits for partners or anti-discrimination practices. If you feel you have been discriminated against, have a look at the sites in **Where next?** at the end of this chapter.

Graduate recruitment

A lot depends on the industry and the individual organisation concerned. In the media and some parts of the public sector, for example, the proportion of gay men who are 'out' at work is significant. However, in other, traditionally more 'macho', industries, such as construction or engineering, it is generally much harder to be openly gay.

But support is out there. The Trades Union Congress (TUC) and UNISON both offer support and targeted advice on work rights—and there is a wealth of gay and lesbian associations linked with professions, trade unions and most large organisations. For example, the armed forces and the police both have their own lesbian and gay associations.

Sexual orientation is included in most equal opportunities statements. So, mentioning on your CV that you were the events organiser or secretary for your university lesbian and gay society *shouldn't* be a problem, although you'll find plenty of people who don't agree with this point of view. Ultimately, disclosure is your choice.

WHERE NEXT?

General

Advice Guide (a source of information run by the Citizens Advice Bureau, packed with advice about a wide range of subjects including discrimination and civil rights): **www.adviceguide.org.uk**

Business in the Community (a collection of UK companies committed to ethnic diversity and other social issues in the workplace): **www.bitc.org.uk**

Change the face of construction (a campaign to promote diversity within the construction industry): www.change-construction.org

Department of Trade & Industry (DTI): **www.dti.gov.uk**

Visit doctorjob.com for advice on your rights:

doctorjob.com/equalopportunities/advice

DTI employment tribunals website:

www.employmenttribunals.gov.uk

National Statistics (research and statistics into national trends):

www.statistics.gov.uk

TARGET Chances (unique events for female, ethnic minority and LGBT students interested in finance, law, the civil service and real estate): **www.targetchances.com**

Trades Union Congress (TUC): **www.tuc.org.uk**

Gender

Equal Opportunities Commission: **www.eoc.org.uk**

Women and Equality Unit: **www.womenandequalityunit.gov.uk**

Work–life Research Centre: **www.workliferesearch.org**

Disability

Action for Blind People: **www.afbp.org**

Blind in Business (a UK charity giving visually impaired graduates practical help to achieve professional careers): **www.bbact.org.uk**

British Computer Association of the Blind: **www.bcab.org.uk**

British Deaf Association (aims to develop pride, identity and awareness of the rights and responsibilities of deaf people): **www.britishdeafassociation.org.uk**

British Dyslexia Association (BDA): **www.bdadyslexia.org.uk**

British Stammering Association (BSA): **www.stammering.org**

Diabetes UK (formerly the British Diabetic Association): **www.diabetes.org.uk**

Disability Rights Commission: **www.drc.org.uk**

Dyslexia Institute: **www.dyslexiaaction.org.uk**

Employers' Forum on Disability: **www.employers-forum.co.uk**

Employment Opportunities: **www.opportunities.org.uk**

Epilepsy Action: **www.epilepsy.org.uk**

Mind (a mental health charity that campaigns for a better life for everyone experiencing mental distress): **www.mind.org.uk**

Motor Neurone Disease Association: **www.mndassociation.org**

Muscular Dystrophy Group: **www.muscular-dystrophy.org**

National Bureau for Students with Disabilities: **www.skill.org.uk**

Remploy (a UK-based supplier of employment opportunities for disabled people): **www.remploy.co.uk**

Royal National Institute for Deaf People (RNID): **www.rnid.org.uk**
Royal National Institute for the Blind (RNIB): **www.rnib.org.uk**
Terrence Higgins Trust (the UK's leading HIV and AIDS charity):
www.tht.org.uk

Age

Age Positive: **www.agepositive.gov.uk**
Campaign Against Age Discrimination in Employment:
www.caade.net
The Employers Forum on Age: **www.efa.org.uk**
EU Employment Directive (Article 13): **www.europa.eu.int**

Race, religion and ethnicity

Black and Asian Grad: **www.blackandasiangrad.ac.uk**
Commission for Racial Equality (CRE): **www.cre.gov.uk**
Institute of Race Relations (IRR): **www.irr.org.uk**
Minority Rights Group International: **www.minorityrights.org**
Workpermit.com (advice on immigration laws worldwide):
www.workpermit.com

Sexual orientation

Armed Forces Lesbian and Gay Organisation: **www.aflaga.org.uk**
CityPink (a network aimed at gay professional women):
www.citypink.co.uk
Gay Business Association: **www.gba.org.uk**
International Lesbian and Gay Association: **www.ilga.org**
Lesbian and Gay Lawyers Association: **www.lagla.org.uk**
Stonewall (campaign group for all lesbian and gay discrimination
issues): **www.stonewall.org.uk**

GETTING INTO
AND GETTING OUT
OF DEBT

GETTING INTO DEBT

Graduate debt has doubled in the last five years, so you'll need to know how to manage your money in the real world more than ever before.

Let's face it, debt is the bugbear of more or less every student and graduate across the land these days. Unless your parents are loaded, you're likely to come out of university with a pile of debt—be that with the beloved student loans company, credit card companies or your not-so-local bank. Here's some info on the different people and organisations who you might end up owing money to.

THE STUDENT LOANS COMPANY (SLC)

As if you didn't know, this is the company to whom pretty much every student in the land is indebted. Well, kind of.

The SLC is actually owned entirely by the UK government, and acts according to the policies put in place by its ministers. The SLC website is filled with really detailed info about repaying your loans, but here are some little tips that should help you on your way.

If you started your course on or after 1 September 1998 . . .

1   You are liable to start paying off your loan the April after you graduate and when your gross income (i.e. what you earn before they take off tax and National Insurance) exceeds £1,250 a month (which is £288 a week, or £15,000 a year). (NB these figures may change, but they are correct at the time of writing)

2   Rather handily (or sneakily, depending on your point of view), the majority of borrowers have their repayments taken straight from their salary. Basically the taxman and the SLC will tell your employer how much to deduct from your salary. These repayments go to the SLC at the end of the tax year, and the SLC credit your loan account.

3   If your salary ever falls below the £1,250 monthly limit, no repayments will be collected for that particular month.

4   It's not like a lot of bank loans—repayments are not over a fixed period. Repayments are worked out as a percentage of your income (currently nine percent) above the £1,250 threshold. Basically, if you earn loads, you'll pay it off much more quickly.

5   The interest rate is based on inflation and will be added to your account every month, based on the amount that you still owe.

BANKS

The banks wooed you with promises of railcards and music vouchers, gave you a little plastic card and now they are probably the major source of your debts.

Graduate loans

Frequently, these loans have rates of interest much lower than normal personal loans, and can be good places to transfer debts that are incurring higher charges, such as large credit card bills that you are unable to pay off. They might also be good for all that 'just started a new job' expenditure, such as a new suit, car or deposit for a room.

You may be advised to take a graduate loan to help consolidate your debts, but make sure you can afford the repayments—a graduate earning the national average starting salary (reportedly around £20,000, though for most of us it will be around £15,000) can ill afford an extra £200 a month to go out of their account. Besides, an interest-free overdraft should be available to you for some time yet. This is a cheaper place for you to store your debt (as long as you make some effort to reduce it).

FIVE FACTS ABOUT GRADUATE LOANS

1 They are usually available up to two years after graduation and may be repaid over terms of up to seven years.

2 You can take a small loan when you finish your studies, and top this up at a later date if you need access to more money.

3 Many banks allow you to borrow up to £10,000 or even £15,000, with APRs of six or seven percent (which is reasonably low).

4 You can also pay extra for loan protection, so that your payments will be met if you find yourself out of work for reasons beyond your control.

5 Most banks allow you to defer payment on a new graduate loan for a short period. Remember, interest will be charged during this period and added to the loan.

Overdrafts

Most banks with graduate accounts offer diminishing overdraft limits after graduation, though they will be flexible. You might, for example, have a £2,000 authorised overdraft some years after graduation, for which you could pay a monthly flat rate (rather than varying amounts of interest).

If you are prone to running out of money at the end of the month, be wary of your overdraft limit! You could incur charges for going over the agreed limit, and the APR on unauthorised borrowing is pretty steep (as high as 29 percent).

It's easy to extend overdrafts these days; so be wary of building up debts that you can't afford. Don't make a habit of extending your overdraft every month—work with your bank to organise a structure to pay it off over time, and reduce its limit.

When your other debts are out of the way, try to reduce your overdraft. It's easy to think of it as 'your' money. It ain't.

Personal loans

Much like graduate loans, these can be for any amount (usually up to £15,000) and can be paid off over periods of up to ten years. Loans like these can be secured (tied to your house) or unsecured. If you fail to make the payments on an unsecured loan you could be credit blacklisted. If you default on a secured loan, you, err, don't have a house any more.

> **Remember to compare financial products! There are lots of useful websites to help you make sure you're getting the best deal.**

As with all things financial, you need to get the best deal, so shop around. Try to compare APRs, but make sure you are comparing like with like, as lenders sometimes calculate them in different ways. Rates could vary from 7 to 20 percent. The shorter the term of the loan, the less you will pay in interest charges. There are a lot of disreputable loan companies out there, so deal only with companies on the Office of Fair Trading's list of licensed lenders.

CREDIT CARDS

Everybody knows how easy they are to get and, unfortunately, a lot of people also know how easy it is to rack up a pile of debt in a very short space of time.

To avoid trouble, you need to control your spending and feel comfortable paying off the full amount as often as possible. The golden rule: try to use your credit card for one-off big purchases. If you find yourself usingyour credit card for essentials, especially your weekly food shopping, you might end up in a spot of bother.

If you're confident that a credit card is worth the trouble, you need to shop around for the best deal. It's likely that you will have to pay a minimum every month, which could be a flat charge or a percentage of the outstanding balance. Credit limits will vary as well. You might be tempted by a large credit limit, but will you be able to pay it off, and can you afford the interest? Bear in mind that it is a credit *limit*, not a *target*.

FIVE CREDIT CARD TIPS

1   Analyse your spending habits to get the right card for you. If you intend to pay off the full amount every month, interest charges don't matter. Instead, look for cards with no annual fee, a decent 'grace' period before you have to pay the bill, and that offer loyalty points, cashback and the like.

2   If you know you can't clear the full amount every month, shop around for cards with low rates. But remember that cards with low interest rates may have high charges for late payment or going over your credit limit.

3   It is easy to be confused when shopping around for the best deal—try to compare the Annual Percentage Rate (APR) (i.e. like against like). A typical APR could be between 13 and 17 percent.

4   Some credit cards have interest-free joining periods—although only use these if you are confident of paying off the debt within the interest-free period.

5   Credit cards are good for large purchases because the credit card company is liable along with the seller in case of a breach of contract. So, if anything happens—the firm goes bust or you don't receive your goods—you should get your money back.

Store cards

Avoid store cards if at all possible, however tempting a ten percent discount on your first purchase might be. Some store cards have an APR as high as 30 percent. You will need to be very disciplined to ensure that you pay off purchases within the interest-free period before the APR kicks in, otherwise you could pay well over the odds for your new jeans. Be sure to check the APR before signing up—most credit cards have APRs of less than 18 percent, so you're usually better off putting your shopping on one of these.

FRIENDS AND FAMILY

If you can, and before you get into serious money troubles, turn to your mates or your relatives.

You may need to borrow small amounts to get you through to the end of the month, or larger sums to help you to manage other debts (usually with higher rates of interest than those charged by your mum). Whatever the amount, it is important that you treat this debt seriously. When you borrow from those close to you, you risk emotional strains to you and your relationships.

FIVE THINGS TO REMEMBER ABOUT BORROWING MONEY FROM YOUR MATES

1 As soon as you think there might be a problem paying it off, let them know. They'll appreciate not being left in the dark.

2 Lending money to people is a very sensitive issue—remember that it will have an impact on the lenders too. They may have budgeted for you to pay it back within a certain time.

3 If you have other, seemingly more important, debts, it's tempting to let the debt lie, maybe in the vain hope that they'll forget about it! Try to avoid this by paying off a small amount every month by direct debit.

4 Your friend and family 'bankers' might not take kindly to ostentatious spending on non-essentials like new clothes.

5 Agree a repayment structure, possibly involving interest payments too. Both parties could be winners, as you end up paying a lower rate of interest and they could get a higher rate than the bank offers on their savings.

TAKING CONTROL

So you're about to graduate with debts of £15K?

You start to investigate careers and find that investment banks pay £35K. On a salary like that you could be back in the black by Christmas.

Then someone tells you that the government is wiping clean student loans for newly qualified teachers in shortage subjects. How sweet of them! That's you sorted, then.

You dash off applications to City banks and PGCE courses and prepare to live happily ever after, smug and debt free.

STOP! This is sheer fantasy, and bears no resemblance to real life and real work. Those pesky recruiters and admissions tutors will see through your motives right away.

And even if you do manage to persuade both the tweedy teachers and the pinstriped bankers that you have the skills and motivation for their lines of work, you'll get a nasty shock on your first day at work. Needing highly-paid work to pay off your debts is no guarantee you'll get it—and even less of a guarantee that you'll enjoy it.

On the other hand, your debts exist in the real world too, and today's graduates literally can't afford to be picky about career choice—some compromise may be necessary. The trick is to make a balanced and realistic decision about the situation. This won't be easy, but here are some nuggets of wisdom to help you.

---

10 STEPS TO TAKING CONTROL OF YOUR FINANCES

1   Make sure you get a job whose salary matches your capacity to spend. Or maybe one with a generous 'golden hello' for paying off debts.

2   Budget right from the start. However tempting it is to blow your first salary packet, don't. As soon as you know your outgoings and how much you will take home each month, work out a budget, setting aside part of your salary to pay off your debts?

3   If you're really struggling with your cash, keep a daily record of your expenditure. You'll soon notice where the money is going, and identify the areas where you need to cut back. And don't forget to check your bank statements carefully.

4   Avoid getting into even more debt—which means not running out of money before pay day. Try to put some money aside to help cover you for unexpected expenses. If you're struggling

on a low starting salary, try at the very least to keep your debt stable until you can afford to start paying it off.

5   Manage your own expectations. Getting out of debt won't happen overnight, so think long term and set yourself realistic targets in the short term. It may help to live with your parents for a short while, to make inroads into your debt.

6   If you get a windfall or bonus, put it towards paying off your debts. Avoid the temptation to blow it on a holiday/car/gambling spree.

7   Forget about your student loan for the time being. Credit reference agencies don't pay attention to your debts to the Student Loans Company, so they aren't a priority. And you're probably automatically paying it off, whether you want to or not.

8   Pay your biggest and most expensive debts off first. Remember that credit and store cards are the worst forms of debt—you'll run up nasty debts too quickly and be charged high interest rates.

9   Think about consolidating your debts and transferring them to a credit card with lower interest charges—some have introductory rates of 0 percent.

10 Remember that bankruptcy is a last resort. You may have read in the press about bankruptcy being an option these days, but the disruption to your life may not be worth it.

SOURCES OF HELP

It's tempting to keep borrowing in the hope that one day you will be earning enough for it to magically disappear. But debts only disappear when you think about them seriously and realistically. So, without further ado, here's a quick run through of who to turn to when things get hairy.

Bank manager

If you get into financial difficulties, the first port of call should be your bank. The key, as ever, is to be open with them. Let them know if you think you're going to go over your overdraft limit or if you're struggling to keep up payments on your credit card. They will be happy to talk you through your options and offer solutions.

The bank manager as perhaps your parents knew him (it was invariably a 'him') is most definitely a thing of the past, and it's much more likely that you'll be talking to different people about your overdraft, your graduate loan and about your account in general; so things can get a bit confusing. Even though they try to sell you their financial wares so that they have you and your money for longer, they do generally know what they're talking about.

Citizens Advice Bureau (CAB)

An old favourite, the CAB is a registered charity staffed with volunteers, offering independent (and free) advice on debt and consumer issues, as well as anything to do with benefits, housing, employment or immigration. Search for details of your local CAB online, and then drop in or phone to talk about your options and your legal rights. The CAB website has an advice guide which includes info on how to negotiate with creditors.

Consumer Credit Counselling Service (CCCS)

The CCCS provides independent, free counselling on personal finance and realistic strategies to pay off debts. There is loads of info on the CCCS website, including a 'debt check' and an 'ask a counsellor' section, plus links to further help.

Debt management agencies

Be wary of paid-for debt management companies. These are organisations that reschedule debt through negotiations with creditors, so that monthly payments are reduced. Very often they will take the first debt repayment as their fee, along with a 15 percent monthly VAT charge, and other interest charges too. Loan consolidators are also to be treated with caution—often these recommend taking out one loan, usually with high interest, to pay off all other debts. These loans may be secured (tied to your property) and are a riskier business than the debts they're designed to pay off.

Family

Your parents may have funded you through university, and may be quite unaware of the debts you have built up over the years. But the great thing about family is that they should understand. They can be a good source of advice—parents will have more experience of dealing with banks, managing overdrafts and generally handling and saving money. That said, they might be a bit out of touch with the financial realities of being under 25 in the 21st century.

Independent financial advisers (IFAs) and insolvency practitioners (IPs)

IFAs can help if you're feeling a bit confused about your money and the different financial offers available. If you speak to them in person they can find out the precise details of your situation, and advise accordingly. The thing to remember is that you needn't pay for financial advice. If you do pay, make sure the adviser is authorised by the Financial Services Authority (FSA) or is a member of R3. Find out exactly what the person stands to gain from the advice they give (e.g. exorbitant fees or commission for selling a financial product). This should help you decide whether or not to take their advice.

National Debtline

Specifically for people with debt problems in England, Wales and Scotland, the National Debtline offers free, independent advice over the phone. They can also help you to set up a debt management plan for free. Their advisers are well trained and should be able to talk you through your options.

Payplan

Payplan is another free advice service—supported by the National Debtline and commercial organisations—which offers face-to-face consultations and debt management plans. Creditors pay Payplan nine percent of the money it recoups on their behalf. The website has a useful debt calculator, which prompts you to think about your outgoings and your income, and works out how much money you have left every month with which to tackle your debts.

Student welfare

If you're still a student or have recently graduated, your student union welfare office might be able to help with advice and some even award mini-grants and loans. Check your student union website for more details.

Bankruptcy Advisory Service

These are the people to contact if things are a bit more serious. Bankruptcy should not be considered unless there really is no other alternative.

WHERE NEXT? ✔

Bankruptcy Advisory Service (01482 633034/633035):
www.bankruptcyadvisoryservice.co.uk

Citizens Advice Bureau (CAB): **www.citizensadvice.org.uk**

Consumer Credit Counselling Service (0800 3281813/1381111):
www.cccs.co.uk

doctorjob.com's complete guide to managing debt:
doctorjob.com/debt

Moneyfacts.com (use this site to compare different graduate bank accounts and loans): **www.moneyfacts.com**

National Debtline (0808 808 4000): **www.nationaldebtline.co.uk**

Office of Fair Trading: **www.oft.gov.uk**

Money Supermarket: **www.moneysupermarket.com**

Payplan (0800 0854 298): **www.payplan.com**

Student Loans Company (0870 242 2211): **www.slc.co.uk**

ORGANISING ACCOMMODATION

GETTING STARTED

No matter how hutch-like, dilapidated and rat-infested it is, there is always some sort of deeply-felt tie to your first non-student home.

Council tax, contracts, deposits—they're all yours now, and that's before we even get onto the assortment of degenerates you'll end up sharing with. It's not all gloom, though. Having your own house (either rented or, if you're lucky, bought) can offer you the freedom you've wanted since leaving home but never quite got as a student, tied down by homework, guilt and cheap beer. You probably won't spend as much time in your house as you did when you were a student, but for some reason that makes it feel more like home.

So what do you need to know? Firstly, think about the kind of area you want to live in—are you willing to accept that a cheaper house may mean witnessing carjacking and ungodly urban brutality on a regular basis? You might want to be close to work to cut down on that all-important commuting time. Alternatively, you might decide that you just can't live unless you're near a quality record shop. It's important to be flexible, though—the right kind of accommodation in the right area at the right price is unlikely to fall into your lap at this stage.

Timing is important. In general, you should start househunting three to four weeks before you want to move in.

The property type will obviously also be important—do you want to take a gamble and house share or can you afford to rent on your own? Do you want to get furnished or unfurnished? Do you want to get a flat, a house, a studio apartment (dahling) or a skanky bedsit?

When viewing a property, always take someone with you. Don't let yourself be rushed, and inspect everything carefully—appliances, fittings, cupboard space, toilet facilities, neighbours. Find out exactly what's included in terms of things like furniture, garden use and parking spaces.

Home is where the heart is

Right, it's deposit time, but don't be afraid. A landlord can't by law charge you more than one sixth of the annual rent, and it's likely to be in the region of a month's rent. A deposit is levied to protect the landlord from unreasonable acts of wastage or damage by tenants—it's important to make the distinction between this and reasonable wear and tear. Your deposit could be withheld if you fail to replace or repair damaged items of furniture, if you leave with outstanding debts, or, most commonly, if you fail to leave the property in a clean and tidy state. (If you rented as a student, you'll no doubt have experience of this already.)

The big day has arrived, and you've remembered to pack the kettle where you can find it, but what else should you remember? Always take readings of gas and electricity on your first day. Read your contract thoroughly, and get a copy of everything that you have signed. You should also make sure that you have a complete inventory of current fixtures and fittings. Remember—failing to question anything you don't agree with could cost you big-time later on.

You're happy in your new home, but then it starts leaking sewage into your bedroom. What can you do? Your landlord should be responsible for fixing the structure of the house, together with water, gas, electricity, sanitation and heat installations. You can expect to wait up to 21 days for non-urgent repairs, but a threat to health or a great inconvenience should be seen to within a couple of days. If it isn't, write a letter to your landlord, and then send a second letter by recorded delivery if that fails. There are three main last resorts:

1   Using the local Environmental Health Department to take action.
2   Taking the landlord to court.
3   Using the rent to pay for repairs (as long as you follow the right procedure).

If you need further advice about housing problems, there are several resources available. Many areas have a local authority housing aid centre, which can advise on all housing problems, while law centres will dispense free legal advice and could even represent you in court. The Housing Act 1988 protects you from harassment from your landlord (e.g. verbal abuse, or letting himself into your room to go through your things), while the Protection from Eviction Act 1977, err, protects you from eviction.

Moving in

So you've spent days trying to find a place. Endless phone calls and rearranged appointments. Polite conversations with people you wouldn't dream of moving in with, and polite comments about houses you wouldn't dream of moving into: 'Oh no, it's not the cat wee or the rubbish piled by the front door, I'm just looking for something a little bit more roomy.' Shyster landlords, most of them couples in their thirties who think that having a few properties makes them special.

Then comes the move itself—as you bundle your belongings into the boot of a friend's car ('I never knew I had so much stuff') or hire a dodgy white van and brave the roads. A word of advice: make sure you know what the insurance rules are and how to drive them before you head off into the sunset.

You'll want to make your new home perfect, so no doubt there'll be the nightmare that is a visit to IKEA. Soon your new abode will be kitted out with stylish-but-flimsy bits of furniture with stupid names and your life will be complete. It's inevitable that your old housemates will plague you with outstanding bills for the next six months, on top of the bills for your new place, and you'll have to tell everyone (friends, colleagues, banks, pension companies, magazines that you subscribe to, mobile phone operators, debt collectors) that you've moved too.

Housemates

Housemates come in many guises. If you're lucky you'll all get on like a house on fire. You'll go for drinks on Wednesdays and watch *Hollyoaks* together on Sunday mornings. You'll be honest and frank with each other, there won't be any lingering tensions and you'll all go to bed early. Being realistic, though, if you've landed yourself in a house full of strangers it's likely that at least one of them could have issues of one kind or another.

You might experience the *evil housemate*, for example—she who phones Argentina every day for a month and then disappears before the colossal bill arrives. Or maybe you'll come into contact with the *nutter housemate*—the one who stays out until 3am on a Tuesday night, then comes home pumped full of narcotics and has an impromptu party in the hall. Now that you need your sleep, these things will start troubling you. Then there's the *dirty housemate*—the one who hardly washes, leaves all his washing up and deposits curly ginger hairs in the sink. Nice.

Mostly, though, your housemates will just provide you with a succession of minor irritations. The one who talks on the phone for hours and never gets round to paying the phone bill. The one who's always right about everything. The one who won't talk to you for a week after you came home late on Saturday night and woke her up. The one who spends hours in the shower and uses up all the hot water. And there's always one who moves his girlfriend in 'just for a couple of days', which turn into three months.

You should view annoying housemates philosophically. Unless they're complete psychopaths, you can probably live with their quirks. You might have to speak up if it comes to unpaid bills and mounting washing up, but it's no use letting them get to you. There are always going to be things that wind you up about living with other people. If you put four or five people in an enclosed space for any period of time, some sort of tension is bound to arise. Unless you've got enough cash to get a place of your own, you'll probably be stuck with housemates for a few years yet. Besides, if you got rid of them you'd have to come home to an empty house every night. And that might just get a little bit depressing.

Council tax

Council tax is the money each household pays to finance local authority services such as education, social services, the fire brigade, roads, libraries, museums and rubbish disposal to name but a few. This tax is payable by most non-students aged over 18. The amount depends on the market value of the property, how many people are resident and any benefits the residents may be entitled to, and will vary from one authority to another. To find out more you should contact your local authority.

There is one council tax bill for each dwelling, whether it is a house, bungalow, flat, maisonette, mobile home or houseboat, and whether it is owned or rented. A 'resident' is a person of 18 years or over who lives in the dwelling as their only or main home. This means that owner-occupiers or resident tenants (including council tenants) usually have to pay the tax. In some cases, more than one person is responsible for seeing that the bill is paid. People who are joint owners or joint tenants are jointly liable.

Council tax is worked out on a daily basis. If you tell your old council about your move it can adjust your bill and make sure that you pay the right amount. This is especially important if you move to a new council area, as you may be due a refund, depending on the method you used to pay the council tax and how much has already been paid. Make sure you keep councils informed about where you're living. You may face a fine if you don't.

The impact of your council tax bill may be reduced by:
✔ discounts (for example, for homes with only one adult)
✔ benefits (for people with low incomes. A leaflet is available from the Department of Social Security)
✔ reductions for disability (for homes adapted for a person with a disability)

New city, new life

So what does life in a new city hold for you, apart from myriad opportunities to get utterly lost the first time you have a beer two streets from your new house? It can be quite stressful getting to know a new place, given that you'll now be out at the office during the day, which dramatically cuts down the time you have to acclimatise yourself. Without some sort of initial effort, you might find yourself knowing only your immediate area, the route to work and the town centre if you're lucky. Perhaps you know someone in your new home town who could show you the ropes. As a minimum, you ought to demand a tour of pubs and nightspots from your new work- or house-mates.

Staying in your university town

I know what you might be thinking: living in university town + having money = fantastic life as an über-student. What you may have failed to take into account is that university town = university + town. In simple terms, you're not a student any more, and if you want to stay in the same town and live a satisfying life, you're going to have to get used to this pretty quickly.

You might expect to be able to live as a working type by day and then a vicarious student by night. However, factors such as socialising at work, working late, the inability to go out on a nine-hour bender on a Tuesday afternoon and fundamental differences in terms of common experience are likely to significantly reduce the amount of time you can feasibly spend with your student mates. Another problem with the vicarious student life is that wherever you go in the town, there will be students everywhere (some of whom you might even know) forcefully reminding you that it is they, not you, who are still students, and yes, the grass is greener on campus, thank you very much.

Of course, you'll still be in touch with your old friends, and you should make new friends at work too; so staying in the same town for your first job can be an excellent way to ease yourself into the working world. You won't have any of the added stress of getting to know the town. As long as you don't get complacent, knowing the town but approaching it from a completely different angle could give you a fresh view of the places you once knew and loved as an eighteen-year-old innocent abroad.

WHERE NEXT?

IHaveMoved.com (a handy service that takes the hassle out of changing all your addresses): **www.ihavemoved.com**

27 LOOKING AFTER YOURSELF

HEALTH AND HEALTHCARE

When you're working all the hours God sends and trying to keep your social life up to your student standards, it's crucial that you look after yourself.

There's no need to come over all hypochondriac, but just be aware that long hours cooped up in an over-heated, over-air-conditioned, over-open-planned office with your colleagues' germs will lead to all manner of snuffles and sore throats. In an office there's always 'something going round', particularly in those killer months of January and February. And don't think you're spared by not having an office job. Professions like teaching expose you to even more bugs, and civil engineers battle it out against viruses in their rain-soaked trenches. As for the healthcare professions themselves, well, you don't even want to ask what infections lurk in hospital toilets. The mere thought of them makes your flesh rot.

Then there's RSI and screen fatigue. Your induction should include a brief health and safety talk, clarifying the rules and regulations for your particular job (not to mention things that you'll hopefully never have to do, like how to lift boxes and find the office first aid kit—think Gareth's Health and Safety lesson in *The Office*). If you suffer from any disabilities, even if only a minor eye complaint, you may have rights, such as a special type of computer screen. And if you're lucky, the company will supply regular massages and posture training. You're luckier still if private health care is included as part of your package—although you've probably got to have more than a bad case of the 'flu to make full use of it.

Apart from that, all the normal good advice applies. Get to bed nice and early, eat properly and/or take plenty of vitamin pills. Take regular breaks from the screen, but don't devote them to Mrs Marlboro.

Sick leave and sick pay

With sick pay and sick leave it's very much a case of knowing what you're entitled to. It's a basic legal right to receive sick pay, which will be paid by your employer when you are sick for a period of up to 28 weeks in one spell of sickness. You are entitled to it if you have been sick for at least four days in a row (handily, this includes weekends and bank holidays). Many work contracts stipulate that employees will receive their normal salary when on sick leave, in which case there will be no need for payment of Statutory Sick Pay. It's best to check your contract for details of how your own company deals with these matters.

The rate of Statutory Sick Pay is worked out according to an employee's normal weekly earnings. If your average earnings before deductions such as tax and National Insurance (NI) are no less than £84.00 a week (the amount necessary to be liable to pay National Insurance contributions), the rate of statutory sick pay is £70.05 per week. It's not much, but you probably won't be up to a big spending spree anyway. And you may be eligible for other support, such as housing benefit.

Stress

Entering the world of work can be stressful enough, but combine the early mornings and rush-hour traffic with deadlines, demanding clients and presentations and you could come close to a complete nervous breakdown. Fret not; stress can actually improve productivity and performance if maintained at a healthy level. But if you do start to feel irritable and tired, calm yourself with some proven methods of unwinding from the tensions of the day.

The key is to put your worries into perspective and take the time to de-stress.

Aromatherapy, deep breathing and massage in any form—from your head to your feet—are popular means of relaxing, but more unusual ideas include playing with a yo-yo or focusing on a brightly coloured dot somewhere in the room and emptying your mind of all your worries. Alternatively you could close your eyes and imagine yourself in an exotic location. Now listen to the rhythm of the waves and feel the sun on your face, as you write your problems in the sand and watch the waves wash them away. Feeling better yet? A more extreme idea is to write a list of everything that is bothering you and then burn the list. Don't try this in the office, though. It may have the opposite of the desired effect.

WHERE NEXT?

Department for Work and Pensions (DWP; essential info about statutory sick pay):
www.dwp.gov.uk/lifeevent/benefits/statutory_sick_pay.asp
International Stress Management Association (ISMA; look here for plenty of stress-busting top tips): **www.isma.org.uk**
Manage Stress (practical advice and a stress quiz):
www.manage-stress.org.uk
Repetitive Strain Injury Association: **www.rsi-uk.org.uk**
Stress UK (an authoritative guide to all things from legal issues to therapies and therapists): **www.stress.org.uk**
Statutory Sick Pay Act 1994:
www.opsi.gov.uk/acts/acts1994/Ukpga_19940002_en_1.htm
Stress-busting animation, cartoon capers and games galore:
www.stressederic.com

28

YOU GET A JOB . . . AND YOU HATE IT. WHAT NOW?

FIRSTLY: YOU'RE NOT ALONE

Many graduate recruits feel let down in the first months of their first job. Is this really the job described in the glossy brochure? Is this really what I spent all those years at university for? Or worse, is this the rest of my life?

The answer to all of these questions is invariably 'no'. Employers have become increasingly concerned in recent years about how to manage graduates' expectations of the job. Some have succeeded to a greater or lesser degree. There's certainly been a trend towards more honesty and thus self-selection on the part of graduates; so the job shouldn't come as too much of a shock.

50% In a survey of more than 2,000 graduates aged 21–45, half said they 'often feel bored at work'.

Source: graduate tedium index, quoted in the *Guardian*, July 2006

On the other hand, when you've jumped through so many hoops and tried so darn hard to land that job, it's almost inevitable that your glasses are going to get a teensy bit rose-tinted. Hating your shiny new graduate job is therefore still a common problem. It's also completely normal to feel a little out of your depth in the first year—especially if you're working in one of those chuck'em-in-at-the-deep-end organisations.

Secondly: Don't rush into anything

Take a deep breath and try to stand back from the daily grind. Work out exactly what it is you don't like. Is it the intrinsic nature of the work, the company culture, your immediate colleagues or boss? Consider how it differs from your expectations. Then try to investigate how realistic it is that any of these factors will change. If you're on a rotating graduate programme or a cycle of short projects, for example, it's probably worth sticking it out until the next assignment. Even if you're not in this position, it may be worth giving things time to improve. After all, you can't expect generous helpings of responsibility and a jet-setting lifestyle in your first few months. Or perhaps this is the problem—too much too soon. If so, it will definitely get easier with time, and there may be additional support or training available to you.

Ask yourself whether it's the actual day-to-day work that makes you want to move, or if the problem is with other issues. Take a look at the list below, see if your own issue is among them, and then consider whether it might in fact be possible to turn the situation around.

✔ **Not getting on with your boss.** This is the number one reason people cite for leaving their jobs. If your manager is nasty, abusive, bullying or controlling, there might not be much you can do about it. However, if the situation is more subtle—the manager fails to involve you in decisions about your work, never shows appreciation, or omits to develop your talents and abilities, for example—you should try talking to him or her. Many people don't realise the effect they have on others. If you feel as if you need some back-up you could ask a more senior manager to have a word, or maybe the HR department could intervene. Alternatively, what are the options for you to move to another department or report to a different manager?

✔ **Feeling stuck.** If your current position offers no hope of promotion and you see no obvious evidence of other work that you might like to do instead, there are still avenues to explore. Most organisations value initiative and people who want to continue to develop and learn, so talk to your manager about opportunities for lateral moves or particular assignments that will stretch your skills. Or perhaps you might find a colleague who feels the same way as you do—how about swapping jobs?

✔ **Feeling unappreciated.** Sadly, this is very common. If you never receive any recognition for your efforts, try telling your manager that you would value his or her input, or ask for regular feedback sessions (be prepared for both good and bad) so you can improve. If the issue revolves around money, trying asking for a pay rise, backing up your request with plenty of evidence for why you deserve one. If a rise isn't forthcoming immediately, ask for a review at a future date or see if you can get agreement for a performance-linked one. Then make sure you perform!

✔ **Feeling overworked.** In these days of reduced resources and lean teams, it's quite likely that you are overworked. Collect evidence to back up any claim that your job involves more than one person can reasonably handle, and then discuss the situation with someone who can do something about it. Possible options include employing someone else to help you, identifying tasks that you could stop doing or delegate to someone else and analysing where you might be able to work more efficiently.

✔ **Disliking your employer, colleagues or customers.** You're never going to love everyone you work with, so it's worth checking your own attitude first. Can you maintain a courteous, professional relationship and keep your personal feelings out of it? Are there steps you can take to reduce your exposure to people you find difficult? (You don't have to spend your lunch break around colleagues who complain constantly, for example.) Could you move to a different part of the organisation?

Whatever the case, don't slip into 'grass is greener' syndrome. Especially after a Friday night in a bar with your mate's boyfriend, Bullshit Barry. No-one's job is that good.

Thirdly: Talk to someone in the organisation

If you genuinely feel that the job has been misrepresented to you, you should take it up with your manager at an early stage. There could have been communication problems at some point in the recruitment process. And they can't do anything about these problems if they don't know about them.

But if it's more of a vague feeling of dissatisfaction or doubt, talk first to a mentor, a buddy or a friendly colleague a year or two further down the line than you. They should be able to give you an idea of (a) how the job might change for the better or (b) how they found their own attitudes to it shifting in the early days. At least you're free to whinge openly to them, which you can't really do with your manager. Colleagues are also good sources of information on interesting openings within the organisation.

This advice is particularly relevant to those on structured training programmes or professional exam courses, who often end up doing drudge work in the first year, in return for all that free education, not to mention fantastic prospects later in life. Trainee accountants and solicitors take note! But it's also useful to those who feel swamped with the volume of work and responsibility. Colleagues a year or two older will be able to confirm whether or not everything gets easier with practice, or may have developed good strategies for dealing with the stress.

Fourthly: Revise your expectations

However prestigious the job, it's unlikely that you're going to reach the same levels of intellectual satisfaction as you did during your degree. The satisfactions of work may be derived from other sources: creativity, negotiation, convincing a difficult customer. So try and accentuate the positives to yourself and see if you can make the required mindshift to enjoy the job after all.

And finally: If steps 1 to 4 fail, prepare to resign

However hard you try, there are some situations where leaving is your best or only option; life's too short to spend time working in a situation where you really are miserable, and, if it's a question of maintaining your mental health, there's no alternative. The standard advice is not to leave before finding something better. After all, you can use your lunch hours to research other careers on the Internet and your remaining days of leave to attend interviews. You never know; in the meantime things might improve beyond all expectations.

> **The job market can be a cold and lonely place if you're not entirely sure what you're looking for, and simply quitting your job can have implications for your CV and the way you're perceived by potential employers.**

RESIGNING

What a conundrum—if you leave your job soon after starting will it reflect badly on your ability to commit and make a go of things in difficult circumstances? If you stick it out will you end up unhappy, demotivated and disillusioned? And even if you are happy, how long are you supposed to stay in your first job?

The stats tell us that most graduates leave their first job within three years. So if you're inescapably miserable, don't feel bad about quitting. On the other hand, don't believe all that mythology about leaving after two years being good for your CV. Take your own case on its own merits and be as rational as you can about a very emotive issue. Think about whether you've given the job a chance. Consider whether you would still leave if you were offered more money or a promotion to stay. Talk to your manager about your position and career progression (without mentioning your plans for leaving). Decide whether you'll be better off in any new job that's offered you—it's a long way from making recreational job applications to accepting a new post. Above all, try not to resign without having a job, a freelance contract or a well-planned career break to go to.

Whatever you decide, it's important to plan your exit carefully. An elegant exit that keeps relationships intact is always best—you will want a good reference, and you never know when you'll come across former colleagues again.

THREE RESIGNATION METHODS

1 **A spur-of-the-moment decision** made in haste and possibly anger. Can take the form of a tear-stained note and/or an impassioned speech. Never recommended, even if you're sick and tired of the job.

2 **Resigning aloud** needn't be a symptom of attention seeking or high drama, but the most considerate way of letting a respected boss know that you're quitting. It's not recommended, however, if there's lots of bad feeling in the air—you may say something you regret. If you decide to resign orally, work out what you're going to say and then stick to it. Your boss may probe you for more information, which you may or may not wish to discuss, so plan some words for all eventualities. Try not to dwell on the negative aspects of your time at the company and do expect a reaction: your decision may well come as a surprise. Always leave the meeting on a good note, as people remember both the first and last impression you make on them.

3 **A letter of resignation** gives you more time to prepare what you want to say and gives you greater control of your message.

Whichever way you resign, you must always formalise it with a letter. A resignation letter should be printed (not an e-mail) and can be just two lines (preferably on plain paper), and should include: your name, the date, the person it's addressed to, notice of termination of employment, when this is effective from (this will depend on your notice period) and your signature.

If you're leaving in good circumstances and feel that you want to say a little bit more, emphasise the positive. If, however, you're leaving in strained circumstances, resist the temptation to let off steam. Don't get personal. Just because you're leaving, you shouldn't use your letter to tell your boss what you really think of them. Your comments will remain in your personnel file and may come back to haunt you.

Send the letter to your boss, with a copy to the human resources department. It's wise to have the letter lodged in two places so there's less possibility of its getting lost or ignored.

Make sure you prepare for an exit interview. This is a meeting with your boss when you explain your reasons for leaving and you each have a chance to give feedback. Try to make sure that the meeting is constructive and that you don't use it to air opinions that may be damaging—either to those that you are leaving behind, or to your own professionalism and dignity.

WHERE NEXT?

Visit doctorjob.com for advice and help on life after university:
doctorjob.com/workinglife
About Human Resources: **humanresources.about.com**
Anywork Anywhere: **www.anyworkanywhere.com**
Fish4jobs: **www.fish4jobs.co.uk**
Hays: **www.hays-ap.com**
Manpower: **www.manpower.co.uk**
Reed: **www.reed.co.uk**
Workthing: **www.workthing.com**

INDUSTRY PROFILES

ACCOUNTING

Almost every business, whether a giant multinational or self-employed plumber, needs an accountant, and the roles on offer are correspondingly varied.

Accounting as a career option has become a lot more sexy in recent years. This may be partly due to the accounting scandals that have engulfed multinational organisations recently like Andersen, Enron and WorldCom. Away from the headlines, accounting has undergone a massive change: the key areas of work are traditionally managing cash flow and monitoring profit and loss, but these days accountants are increasingly involved with companies' strategic decision making, managing risk and helping to develop the business. The industry's role is increasingly seen as one of providing clients with a whole range of financial services.

'Accountant' is the name given to any professional with a relevant, nationally recognised qualification. Graduates will typically train for three years upon joining an employer before sitting exams to qualify as a chartered accountant. Your employer will often determine which professional qualification you study for—there are over ten to choose from, most having a speciality such as taxation or public sector work.

Jobs include:

✔ **Forensic accounting.** Quantifying losses arising from an incident, such as floods, fires, motor accidents, thefts and earthquakes. Professionals in this field can be involved in a wide range of tasks, from helping to investigate fraud allegations to assessing the financial impact of a disaster. Two main areas of work are litigation support (quantifying loss of earnings for a court case for example) and insurance. The job can involve a lot of travel at short notice, for example to the aftermath of a hurricane.

✔ **Assurance.** The 'traditional' work of auditing, providing an independent review of a client company's accounts. The job of the auditor is to satisfy shareholders that an organisation's financial statements are an accurate representation of their financial position. Information about risks is also gathered and used to help clients make their business more efficient.

- ✔ **Corporate treasury**. Managing cash flows, investing surpluses and controlling financial risks, usually for a large company. Corporate treasurers in an international company pay particular attention to foreign exchange deals and try to minimise the risk of being left out of pocket by fluctuations in the markets, for example. Graduates can either enter treasury directly or become accountants and specialise at a later date.

- ✔ **Corporate finance.** Advising companies on mergers and acquisitions and financing for big projects through loans or selling assets. There are two stages to the work: deal origination, which involves putting deal proposals together for clients; and execution, which means steering the deal through to the signing of contracts. This is a complex and dynamic area with high pay and long hours.

- ✔ **Corporate recovery.** Rescuing ailing businesses, or in extreme cases putting them into liquidation. This area is like management consulting in some respects, but more technical and hands-on, and it demands some specialisation in some aspects of insolvency law. Negotiation with creditors, lawyers and other accountants is a central part of the work.

- ✔ **Tax.** There are two main branches: advising companies on their liability and ways they can minimise it, or working for the Inland Revenue, either in policy or as an inspector. Tax advisory work is a very complicated field and there are many specialist areas, from helping celebrities make the most of their earnings to advising small businesses on their national insurance obligations.

- ✔ **Management accounting.** Encompasses a wide variety of jobs in commerce and industry which involve managing financial systems, reporting and support functions. Management accounting is more concerned with helping managers to make decisions and forecasts about the future, whereas the main thrust of financial accounting is to provide up-to-date, accurate and clear information regarding a company's financial position.

Any degree discipline is accepted, although language skills are in high demand. You'll usually also need good English and maths GCSE grades, plus at least 22 UCAS points and an expected 2:1. Traditionally, public practice firms formed the backbone of the milkround, with university presentations throughout the autumn, application closing dates in December and initial interviews in spring. This timetable is now more flexible and some employers invite applications all year round.

WHERE NEXT?

Association of Chartered Certified Accountants (ACCA):
www.accaglobal.com
The Association of Corporate Treasurers (ACT): **www.treasurers.org**
The Chartered Institute of Management Accountants (CIMA):
www.cimaglobal.com
Chartered Institute of Public Finance Accountancy (CIPFA):
www.cipfa.org.uk
The Chartered Institute of Taxation (CIOT): **www.tax.org.uk**
doctorjob.com Accountancy and Financial Management advice:
doctorjob.com/accountancy

ADVERTISING

In a nutshell, advertising is about promoting and publicising products or services in order to boost sales.

The roles in advertising are numerous, but the main ones are:

- ✔ **advertising creatives** (art directors and copy-writers): work together as a team, the copy-writer writing text ('copy') and the art director coming up with the visuals. The job can involve creating advertising slogans for products, content for leaflets and brochures, scripts for TV or radio ads.
- ✔ **account executive or manager:** mediates between the client and the creatives, communicating the brief and selling the concept.
- ✔ **media planner or buyer:** works for advertising agencies as a consultant, advising clients on which media should be used to best advertise a product or service. They then purchase the advertising 'space' and 'time'.
- ✔ **account planner:** in consultation with the client devises and oversees a media strategy to hit the target audience.

These roles differ greatly and each requires different skills. For example, an advertising copy-writer will need creative writing skills, while a media planner or buyer will need research and negotiation skills—so investigate each position carefully and don't assume that all jobs in advertising are alike; you may be more suited to one type of work than to another.

The advertising industry is populated by the young: according to research from the Institute of Practitioners in Advertising (IPA), 48 percent of all staff are under the age of 30, and a whopping 81 percent are under 40. The same survey found that women make up nearly 50 percent of the industry (but only 32 percent of board directors and 14 percent of chairmen, CEOs and managing directors).

This booming industry has a reputation for being creative, cutting-edge and dynamic. Yet it is also business-focused and commercial, often having to justify advertising spend in terms of the returns it generates for clients. And it can also be a high-pressure sector to work in—after all, you're only as good as your last ad!

Where should I work?

If you want to get into advertising, the UK is one of the best places to do it. London is well-known as one of the two world centres of creative advertising—the other is New York. What's more, two-thirds of international agencies have their European headquarters in London, according to IPA. But there are also opportunities in advertising outside the capital.

Most people working in advertising are employed by creative or full-service agencies, which act for clients to develop and implement campaigns in the media. However, you could also work for a media independent (specialising in media planning) or for a direct mail/marketing agency.

How competitive is it, and how can I get in?

As you might expect, the industry advertises itself extremely well and, with a reputation for being glamorous, creative and exciting, it attracts many graduates. Yet it's smaller than you might imagine from the big noise it makes, which means it's a competitive business to get into. A recent survey by the IPA found that their agencies had only 15,190 employees in 2004.

So how can you get in? Be prepared to work hard. Work experience is invaluable, but you may need to volunteer in order to get it!

As with any popular profession, it's important to get your name out there. And as positions are often filled without being advertised, you can imagine how vital it is to hear about vacancies by word of mouth, or to be recommended by somebody for a position.

If you want to work in advertising, the hard work is often a reward in itself—as well as the glamour, the potential for generous financial rewards, and the chance to work with other young people in an exciting industry.

WHERE NEXT?

doctorjob.com on advertising careers: **doctorjob.com/advertising**
The Ad Forum: **www.adforum.com**
Brand Republic magazine: **www.brandrepublic.com**
World Federation of Advertisers: **www.wfanet.org**

BANKING AND INVESTMENT

So what do investment banks actually do? Well, contrary to popular belief, it has little to do with investing.

The original purpose of an investment bank was to raise capital and to advise on mergers, acquisitions and other corporate strategies. The definition of 'investment banking' has become slightly blurred in recent years due to the range of things they cover, but here is a list of some the things investment banks do:

- ✔ Underwrite and distribute bond and share issues (primary market activity)
- ✔ Buy and sell securities once they have been issued (secondary market activity)
- ✔ Valuation (calculating what a business is worth)
- ✔ Capital structuring (how a company arranges its finances)
- ✔ Mergers and acquisitions (increasing the value of a business by merging or acquiring another company)
- ✔ New issues (ways of raising funds, either through offering securities which must be paid by the company [debt] or by selling shares in the company itself [equity])

In short, investment banks act as the Matrixesque oracle of financial transactions, anticipating movements of the market, advising businesses on their financial and investment choices and helping them to maximise their shareholder value. This translates into an exciting and rewarding environment, but one where hard work is required more than ever.

Of course, companies are not all like-minded in their strategies; each one may have individual ideas about short-, medium- or long-term ways to maximise shareholder value. Recent trends in mergers and acquisitions (M&A) have meant that transactions have increasingly become what's known as consolidation plays or 'bolt-on' acquisitions. In layman's terms this means that organisations are now reluctant to engage in risky ventures that could potentially destroy shareholder value and instead focus on acquisitions that have a strong strategic rationale which is transparent to their investors.

In the ever-changing, fast-paced environment of financial intitutions, graduates must be able to demonstrate flexibility and an openness to new ideas.

Back, middle or front office?
Some investment banks have these divisions, each of which has a different role to play at different stages of the trading process:

✔ the back office provides administrative and support services
✔ the middle office manages risk and IT resources and executes deals and trades
✔ the front office includes sales personnel and corporate finance.

However, these divisions are not set in stone and in some investment banks they will often overlap.

Operations and the backbone
Those working in the back office provide support to the middle and front offices. Much like working backstage in a circus, but juggling accounts and phones instead of fireballs, they aim to ensure a faultless performance. Back office jobs can include settlements and clearances, record maintenance and accounting. Operations professionals try to review processes and develop better systems to maximise efficiency and profitability. While back office staff can get bogged down with slow processing or 'back office crunch' as it's known, the show must always go on—and the fewer dramas the better!

In the middle
The middle office generally acts as a support for the traders in front office. People working in the middle office deal with the confirmation or affirmation process, reconciliations and reporting. They assist with the trader's daily profit and loss figures and are responsible for information technology.

The middle office is the first step in the operations part of the trade cycle. Once a trade has been validated it will move into the hands of back office.

Front facing

While the trading floor is still hectic and fast-paced, the men in stripy suits shouting 'sell sell!' are long gone. It is filled with lots of phones, screens and people (both male and female), all checking the markets and liaising with clients in a buzzing, modern environment. The front office is where the trading takes place and revenues are generated. Traders working in market-making are responsible for buying and selling securities either over the phone or electronically on behalf of their firm or its clients. Traders working in sales deal directly with clients and provide a link between investors and market-making traders. They supply market information and promote new financial ideas to clients.

A life less ordinary

It's fair to say that the world of investment banking is anything but dull. Whether it's back office, operations, middle office or on the trading floor, there is a buzz of activity—selling, trading, speaking to clients, working on reports, attending meetings, giving presentations; it never stops. The attributes common to successful candidates are analytical skills, communication and presentation skills, initiative, entrepreneurial spirit and a pleasant personality, plus the ability to work at full stretch for extended periods. The world of investment banking offers many exciting opportunities, although the pressured environment is certainly not for the timid.

WHERE NEXT?

doctorjob.com banking and investment advice:
doctorjob.com/banking
Financial Times online: **www.ft.com/home/uk**
Financial news online: **www.efinancialnews.com**
The *Economist*: **www.economist.com**

THE CHARITY SECTOR

The charity sector—also known as the non-profit, not-for-profit, voluntary and third sector—encompasses almost every conceivable area of human endeavour, including international aid, education and animal welfare.

Being charitable isn't enough to find a position with a charity. This is a very competitive arena. After all, most people would like to gain that inner glow that comes from helping others on a daily basis. But paid permanent positions are few and far between. Voluntary work can give you valuable experience, but even this can be difficult to obtain in more specialised fields. You will always find a high street charity (such as Macmillan, Oxfam or Marie Curie) looking for unpaid shop assistants, but finding someone to give you experience at an orphaned penguin sanctuary may be trickier.

Charities used to have a reputation for being inefficient and wasteful, and employees were seen as well-meaning but unprofessional. In response, organisations started employing people from the professions and paying them the going rate; as a result a new generation of charity professionals was born. So, although charitable organisations are always on the lookout for graduates with decent business skills, it can be tough breaking into the sector. With the exception of the larger organisations, very few charities can offer well-funded graduate schemes.

Experience and knowledge of the sector is essential to get a foot in the door. Volunteering part-time or full-time will definitely help when it comes to applications, as will a carefully-targeted CV. Think of your experiences in terms of skills such as communication, management, budgeting or IT which could be transferred to the charity sector. The key to success is to build on your knowledge of the area you want to go into and, above all, be prepared to volunteer and get some real experience; so now's the time to consider jobs that aren't all about making money (but have quite a lot to do with raising it).

✔ Advice workers provide information and guidance about a variety of problems.
✔ Charities administrators play a key role in linking organisations, the public and the media.

✔ Charity fundraisers find ways to generate capital through fundraising activities.
✔ Charity campaigners work with the media and PR agencies and lobbies for policy changes.
✔ Homeless workers provide help for the homeless and people with housing problems.

Increasingly in recent times graduates have been drawn to charity and voluntary work because they want to follow a career that reflects their priorities and outlook on life, and help people less privileged than themselves.

Government interest in the voluntary sector over recent years is an indication of its importance to the political agenda. 'More young people have been drawn to international charities, especially post September 11,' says Annie Kelly, a freelance journalist. 'The big aid agencies have been very vocal about the war in Iraq and debt issues, so young people feel a connection with them. And all the anti-war demos have shown that there are a lot of students who feel passionate about international politics.'

Any volunteers?

An estimated 23 million people volunteer annually in the UK alone. To work successfully for a charity you must empathise with its cause. Enthusiasm is essential, as charities are powered by goodwill. While by their very definition charities run on a non-profit making basis, having staff with good business sense and practicality is imperative to their success.

EXPERT ADVICE: THE VOLUNTEERING BUSINESS

Avoiding the do-gooder image

'You have to be passionate about the fact that you enjoy your work. If you're in it just because of some vague notion of helping the poor people, then you can forget it. You've got to have a selfless streak. But you've got to be selfish about your enjoyment of it. I love teaching, I love new cultures and new ideas. I think you can want to help people out, but not really enjoy the process involved.

It's not just a middle-class guilt thing.'

Nik Hartley is director of programmes, Students Partnership Worldwide (SPW).

WHERE NEXT?

doctorjob.com charity advice: **doctorjob.com/charity**

Charity Choice (an online encyclopedia of charities):
www.charitychoice.co.uk

Charity Commission (government regulator of charities in England and Wales): **www.charity-commission.gov.uk**

Charity People (recruitment agency for the non-profit sector):
www.charitypeople.co.uk

Third Sector: **www.thirdsector.co.uk**

UK Fundraising: **www.fundraising.co.uk**

Do-it! (information about UK volunteering opportunities):
www.do-it.org.uk

Graduate training programmes and internships

Cancer Research UK (two-year scheme in its fundraising and marketing department): **www.imperialcancer.co.uk**

Charities Advisory Trust (short internships or early-entry 'advanced' internships of varying length for those who have two-years' work experience post-graduation): **www.charitiesadvisorytrust.co.uk**

Christian Aid (post-graduation internship schemes):
www.christian-aid.org

International Alert (six-month paid internship scheme. Apply up to a year in advance): **www.international-alert.org**

Oxfam (14-month graduate training scheme in its marketing department): **www.oxfam.org.uk**

People and Planet (12-month paid internship):
www.peopleandplanet.org

CIVIL SERVICE AND CENTRAL GOVERNMENT

The Civil Service impacts on every aspect of British life and can offer graduates an enormous range of opportunities, from devising policies that will influence the nation, to working in human resources, marketing or the security service.

The Civil Service is the collective name for a number of government departments and agencies. There are 170 government departments and agencies, each concentrating on a specific service such as education, transport, pensions or fraud investigation. Departments work with the government to formulate policies, while agencies act to implement them.

Departments

A department is usually headed by a minister who is a member of the cabinet and is known as 'secretary of state'. The minister is accountable to Parliament for the work, decisions and actions of his or her department. Once government policy has been decided, the secretary of state must either accept this or resign, as the policies of departmental ministers must agree with those of the government.

The staff of a department, however, will be made up of politically impartial civil servants. A civil servant is a servant of the Crown, which in effect means that he or she is accountable to the government of the United Kingdom, the Scottish Executive or the National Assembly for Wales. A civil servant's first duty, however, is to the minister in charge of his or her department. A change in minister (due to a general election, for example) will not mean a change in staff. Therefore, although the structure and policies of departments may be reorganised by changes in government policy, they will not necessarily be affected by a change in political power.

Non-departmental public bodies (NDPBs)

Non-departmental public bodies are national or regional public bodies, working independently of the ministers to whom they are accountable. There are over 1,000 NDPBs in the UK. Executive NDPBs have administrative, commercial or regulatory functions, while advisory NDPBs are set up by ministers to advise their department.

Executive agencies

The role of an agency is to deliver government services efficiently. They are part of the Civil Service but have the authority to employ their own staff and organise service provision in a way that will best suit their customers' needs. The day-to-day running of an agency is the responsibility of the chief executive, accountable to a minister, who is in turn accountable to Parliament.

RECRUITMENT ROUTES

The main graduate recruitment programme for the Civil Service is the Civil Service Fast Stream.

This is an accelerated learning and development programme that aims to prepare graduates for senior management positions. Fast streamers will experience a series of different placements, each lasting between 12 and 18 months. They are also encouraged to spend time in other departments and in the private sector in order to gain a wide range of experience.

Entry routes into the Civil Service Fast Stream

The Civil Service now markets its careers under three 'business streams'—corporate services, operational delivery and policy delivery. The Graduate Fast Stream includes the following options:

- ✔ Central departments—for all departments except the Foreign and Commonwealth Office
- ✔ Diplomatic Service (Foreign and Commonwealth Office)
- ✔ European Fast Stream—for those who want to follow a career focused on European issues
- ✔ Science and Engineering Fast Stream
- ✔ Department for International Development (DFID) Technical Development option
- ✔ Clerkships in parliament
- ✔ Government Communications Headquarters (GCHQ)
- ✔ Economists' Fast Stream
- ✔ Statisticians' Fast Stream

Graduates can apply to more than one scheme and are able to place their choices in preferential order. The application process itself is fairly intensive. Once you have selected which scheme or schemes you would like to apply for, you will have a number of days to complete each stage of the process, including:

✔ **online self-assessment tests**
✔ **online tests** including a verbal reasoning and numerical reasoning test and a competence questionnaire. Practice tests and further guidance can be found on the Fast Stream website
✔ **application form**
✔ **supervised e-tray test:** a half-day test completed at a regional centre, including a numerical and verbal reasoning test and an e-tray exercise
✔ **one-day assessment centre**

Some options also include a final selection board.

Graduates will need at least a 2:2 in any degree discipline to apply for the Graduate Fast Stream and must generally be a UK national. In most cases your degree subject won't restrict your options, but be aware that you will be up against stiff competition. In total, only 500 graduates are accepted onto the scheme each year, so you must be able to demonstrate an enthusiasm and a commitment to the post you are applying for.

WHERE NEXT?
doctorjob.com on the civil service and central government: **doctorjob.com/civilservice** Fast Stream: **www.faststream.gov.uk** Civil Service Recruitment Gateway website (non-Fast Stream): **www.careers.civil-service.gov.uk**

IT

In-depth knowledge of technical systems is not necessary for a career in IT, but a passion for technology is crucial.

The IT industry is all about providing businesses with the systems and tools to enable them to work efficiently and effectively. It uses technology to assist people in the completion of their tasks and is now considered an essential part of everyday activities. IT is a diverse profession, which offers opportunities for graduates from a wide range of backgrounds. There are jobs in technical areas, such as software engineering and programming, and there are also opportunities in a variety of other areas such as sales, marketing, finance and consultancy. For a graduate who does not have an IT degree, but who does have a strong interest in technology, a career in one of these areas could be the way forward.

Technical know-how

While it is true that some employers will advertise for graduates with specific skills, others will be looking for graduates who have a broad technical knowledge, perhaps gained from studying for a degree in a science, engineering or maths, and who can apply these skills to a commercial environment. Other employers will not necessarily be looking for technical skills at all. This is because there are some jobs, such as IT consultancy, where non-technical skills are considered more important in recruitment. In such cases employers will be looking for candidates who are good at problem-solving and have an interest in the interactions between IT and business. Most of the more specialist knowledge can be learned on the job.

What next?

For non-IT graduates, demonstrating your interest in IT needn't be a challenge. You should be fully aware of how technology can make a difference to commercial success and how it can be applied in a business setting. It is also important to remember that a recruiter is not a mind-reader; so you will need to think about how you can match your skills and knowledge to the job you are applying for.

Completing some relevant form of work experience is a good start, but don't forget that any work experience can help you to demonstrate that you have transferable skills such as problem solving or a working in a team. You could take a course in order to brush up on your IT knowledge, and there are a number of other ways you can increase you employability, such as teaching yourself programming or completing a masters or conversion course.

1   Read relevant publications and attend conferences where possible to keep up to date with the latest developments.
2   Become a member of any technology-focused societies at university.
3   Try to work in IT-related positions in your summer breaks to gain extra skills and demonstrate your commitment to the profession.
4   Make sure that you can demonstrate your awareness of how IT now shapes much of the commercial world.
5   IT recruiters need highly numerate candidates, so if you have non-numerically-based A levels or degree qualifications, make sure you include your GCSE subjects and grades on your CV.

Employers value a balanced workforce because they are aware of the value of different skills and approaches. Not everybody who works in an IT company will be developing products, and it's important to have people who can communicate effectively with clients and explain the technical side of things in layman's terms. Successful applicants come from a wide range of backgrounds, from science and engineering through to languages and the arts.

WHERE NEXT?

doctorjob.com gives you the lowdown on IT and telecoms: **doctorjob.com/IT**
Careers at Microsoft: **www.microsoft.com/uk/careers**
Scenta: **www.scenta.co.uk/scenta.cfm**
The Institute of Engineering and Technology: **www.theiet.org**

LAW

From employment to the environment, life sciences to real estate, lawyers are involved in almost every aspect of life.

The legal profession comprises both solicitors and barristers, with each of these branches subdividing further into a vast number of different specialisms. And if you don't fancy a traditional career path there are plenty of alternatives, such as working for an in-house legal department, as a government or Crown Prosecution Service lawyer, or in a support role (e.g. as a paralegal or barristers' clerk).

QUALIFYING AS A SOLICITOR

1 **Academic stage.** Law degree, or non-law degree plus conversion course (c.4,000 full- and part-time places). Conversion course fees: £1,175–£5,900.

2 **Vocational stage.** Law Practice Course (LPC) run by a variety of institutions (c.8,500 full- and part-time places). LPC fees: £5,900–£9,300.

3 **Practical stage.** Trainee solicitor on a two-year training contract, before taking up a position as an assistant solicitor.

QUALIFYING AS A BARRISTER

1 **Academic stage.** Law degree, or non-law degree plus conversion course (c.4,000 full- and part-time places). Conversion course fees: £1,175–£5,900.

2 **Vocational stage.** Bar Vocational Course (BVC) run by a variety of institutions (c.1,300 full- and part-time places). BVC fees: £8,095–£11,635.

3 **Practical stage.** Pupillage (one year) followed by tenancy.

NB The figures above are subject to change, but accurate at time of writing.

What about the money?

Becoming a lawyer isn't a get-rich-quick scheme. Some leading solicitors' firms will pay their future trainees' LPC fees, and possibly also conversion course fees and/or a sum towards maintenance; however, the vast majority of students will have to make at least some financial investment in their initial training. That said, everyone on a training contract or pupillage receives a salary—in some instances an extremely generous one—and, while lawyers' earnings vary from passable to stratospheric, after a few years in practice most solicitors and barristers can expect to earn a good living.

Opportunities for non-law graduates

Approximately 40 percent of those who become solicitors or barristers each year have degrees in subjects other than law. Recruiters are far more interested in your skills, experience and personal qualities than in what you've studied. Specific degree subjects can be particularly useful in certain areas of law: modern languages are important for practising European law or in firms with international clients; science degrees are useful in intellectual property law; and a mathematics background will give you a head-start in employment, tax and banking law.

After you graduate you'll need to take a one-year conversion course that covers all the key elements of a law degree. These are known as the Common Professional Examination (CPE) or the Graduate Diploma in Law (GDL) and are run by numerous academic institutions throughout the country. Alternatively, for graduates who have not studied law, some institutions offer a two-year masters degree which covers the area in more depth. Once you've completed your conversion course you'll be able to join law students on the next stage of the qualification process: for solicitors, the legal practice course, or, for barristers, the Bar vocational course.

SOLICITOR OR BARRISTER?

Traditionally these professions had very distinct roles. Solicitors were the first point of contact for clients and advised them on the merits of their case—they then referred them to a barrister, who represented them in court.

These boundaries are slowly starting to disintegrate: solicitors can now gain higher rights of audience, allowing them to stand up in court, while in some cases it is possible for clients to approach barristers directly rather than instructing a solicitor first. In addition, a handful of barristers are currently employed in solicitors' practices. For the time being, though, the two remain separate professions and you will have to choose which one to enter.

Your skills

One useful way to go about this is to examine your own skills and working preferences. One very distinctive feature of life at the Bar—and a large part of its appeal—is advocacy. The idea of representing a client in court is exciting, but it's important to be honest with yourself, as your talents in this area will be a make-or-break factor. Are you comfortable speaking in front of large numbers of people? Can you get your point across clearly? Can you think quickly enough to respond to challenges? Are you able to improvise? It's also important that barristers look and act the part—you must be able to inspire confidence by masking your nerves and taking knockbacks in court without showing emotion.

Communication skills are equally important for solicitors, although you won't be quite so much in the limelight. In general, solicitors have a good deal more client contact than barristers and must be able to inspire trust and build a good working relationship. They also tend to engage in team-work to a greater extent than barristers. As a barrister you will often work either on your own or with one or two other senior members of chambers, depending on the type of law you specialise in. In contrast, solicitors (in larger firms) frequently work together in big teams. Could you work with others for hours at a time, day-in, day-out? Or are you better at motivating yourself and working individually or in small groups?

Lifestyle

There's no escaping the fact that both solicitors and barristers sometimes have to work extremely long hours, and all-nighters are not unknown. Many barristers spend a good deal of time travelling to different courts around the country, while solicitors tend to spend more time in their office and operate within a relatively small distance of it. On the other hand, there are probably more opportunities for solicitors than for barristers to travel overseas on business, such as on secondment to an office abroad. There's also the issue of location to consider. The vast majority of barristers' chambers are to be found in major towns and cities, whereas there's a firm of solicitors on the high street of practically every town in the country.

WHERE NEXT?

The Bar Council: **www.barcouncil.org.uk**

doctorjob.com for advice on all your legal options: **doctorjob.com/law**

LawCareers.net weekly newsletter: **www.lawcareers.net/LCNWeeklyFrontPage.aspx**

The Law Society of England and Wales: **www.lawsociety.org.uk/becomingasolicitor/careerinlaw.law**

Law Britannia: **www.lawbritannia.co.uk/Reference.htm**

HOSPITALITY, LEISURE AND TOURISM

Often overlooked for more 'glamorous' jobs, the hospitality, leisure and tourism industry offers good training and salary prospects, early responsibility and attractive perks—and probably a greater variety of jobs to choose from than any other businesses. In fact, it's the world's biggest industry.

From hotel manager to fitness instructor, from chef to events organiser—there's a job for every skill set and personality. Hospitality is a people business, and as long as you thoroughly enjoy implementing as well as improving your strong interpersonal and communication skills, you'll find a fulfilling career in this industry. The choice of areas in which you can work in hospitality, leisure and tourism is huge. These areas include:

adventure tourism	heritage
airlines	hotels
bars, clubs and pubs	public sector
conferences and events	quick-service retail
cruise liners	restaurants
entertainment and leisure	tour operators
food providers	travel agents
health and fitness	visitor attractions

Other perks of working in this industry include:

✔ **Flexibility.** The industry offers plenty of flexibility. During your career you may move from one job area to another in a number of working environments, from offices to holiday parks.

✔ **Qualifications.** There are training opportunities at every level. Usually employers support their staff in taking their career forward through formal training. Many qualifications can be gained while you work, whether it is a general management or a more specialised qualification.

✔ **Rapid career progression**. Whether you start straight from school, college or university, if you demonstrate initiative you will soon be managing your own team and/or projects and, while starting salaries may not always be great, they will increase with every move up the career ladder. It's worth looking at the long-term benefits of a career in the industry.

227

✔ **International opportunities.** The hospitality, leisure and tourism business is a worldwide industry, and so too are the opportunities —many of them with the multinational tour operators and hotel chains.

✔ **Entrepreneurial opportunities.** There are lots of opportunities for starting your own company. This typically happens after people have gained some experience in employment.

✔ **Fun.** The hospitality, leisure and tourism business offers you the chance to do for a living what other people do in their spare time—skiing, playing football, mixing cocktails and cooking are just a few examples. Nevertheless, a job in this area is not a holiday; you have to work hard of course if you want to get anywhere.

✔ **Sociability.** You will struggle to find another job that is as social as one in this field. Not only will you be in contact with a large number of regular and new customers, but you are also likely to work as part of a large team.

WHERE NEXT?

doctorjob.com on the hospitality industry:
doctorjob.com/hospitality
Hotel and Catering Institute and the Institutional Management
Association (HCIMA): **www.hcima.org.uk**
The Journal of Hospitality, Leisure, Sport & Tourism Education
(JoHLSTE):
www.hlst.heacademy.ac.uk/Johlste/index.html
Young Guns competition: **www.cateringforum.com/youngguns**

MANAGEMENT CONSULTING

Management consultants work with senior managers to improve the performance of the client's organisation. Broadly speaking, consultants identify problems and formulate and implement solutions.

Larger consultancies offer a broad range of consulting services and may be split into divisions that each deal with clients in a specific sector of industry, such as energy or telecommunications, for example. Other consultancies specialise in dealing with particular issues; a strategy consultancy, for example, assists senior managers with their business planning, looking at the most appropriate direction for the business to go in the future. There are also a handful of niche consultancies that specialise in a particular industry sector—in many cases, the financial services industry.

Management consultancies work with organisations in both the public and private sectors, often helping them to deal with a major change. Newly privatised companies use management consultants to help them to adapt to working in a competitive environment. Companies formed by the merger of two large organisations might employ management consultants to help to develop a new working culture.

So what's in it for you? Well . . .

- ✔ **A top job.** One of the main attractions of a career in management consulting is that you'll really get to use your brain. Another is that you'll move from project to project, so the work is varied. You'll often have first class prospects for travel and will work with diverse, intelligent colleagues.
- ✔ **Good money.** Embark on a career in management consulting and you'll earn an average of £31k—that's £10k over the average graduate salary. You'll have to work for it though!
- ✔ **Perks.** Management consultancies are generous with the benefits they offer their employees. Things have calmed down a bit in recent years—you might not necessarily get an in-house hair salon in your workplace, but pension schemes, private healthcare, gym membership, golden hellos and season ticket loans are not to be sniffed at!

✔ **Something to build on.** Management consultancy is a great springboard for all kinds of careers. Your training will probably include assignments in different industry sectors; so you'll have plenty of experience to draw on when it comes to making decisions further down the line.

In most consultancies you start as an analyst, a team member. After two or three years you reach consultant level, at which point you are expected to lead your own teams, and possibly even projects. After a further two or three years you become a senior/lead consultant or manager, depending on the organisation. At this level you design and develop solutions, lead engagements and develop future work. After that, you're looking at a director or partner role.

The downside—for some, at least—could be that consultants tend to be based at clients' premises, which means that they may have to spend a good deal of time in daily travel or stay away from home for lengthy periods.

Why apply now?

If you're a finalist, you have to plan your career, and a graduate job in management consulting isn't like holiday work or a second job—early application deadlines are very common (they can even be as early as October). If you're in your penultimate year and looking for an internship, the closing dates for many of these are in February. So get a move on, and prepare yourself well for a very competitive and fairly tough application procedure.

Successful recruits possess a combination of excellent academic results and strong personal skills. A degree in mathematics, accounting or finance is desirable but by no means necessary. You will need to inspire confidence and be tactful yet persuasive. Analytical skills are important since consultants break down problems and construct solutions to them. You will be comfortable analysing large amounts of research information and data, extracting the relevant points. You'll need to learn quickly, work well in a team and have a lively and inquisitive mind.

MEDIA AND PUBLISHING

Publishing, media and the performing arts are amongst the most competitive industries to break into. However, if fame and fortune beckon then this is where you should be looking.

The opportunity for creativity and individuality is one of the most attractive features of this sector of employment, as well as the chance to develop skills acquired through your degree or extracurricular activities such as creative writing or acting. Just a note of warning, however—these industries are commercial working environments where job security is by no means guaranteed.

- ✔ **Publishing** can be sub-divided into four distinct areas: books, magazines, music and online publishing. This industry is particularly attractive to graduates and offers immense job satisfaction, particularly when you see the finished product.
- ✔ The **performing arts** are also dependent on public support—a theatre or concert hall can exist only if it sells tickets! To be honest, it is very difficult to become a professional in any of the performing arts. But the struggle is worth it when you see your name in lights! The key to breaking into this industry is experience, persistence and networking. Oh, and talent, of course . . . and possibly an element of luck.
- ✔ Jobs in the **media** offer exciting possibilities, but the industry is very competitive and any work experience is a valuable asset.

If you do decide that a career in one of these fields is for you, then determination is the key to success. You'll have to persevere and remain optimistic if you want to realise your dream of becoming a famous actress or the next Steven Spielberg.

Work experience in media

The media industry is always very popular with graduates, but unfortunately it is also one of the most competitive to break into. Work experience is crucial if you want to convince employers that you are serious. There aren't many formal structured work experience schemes—the companies which do offer them are generally the large publishing houses or television companies. Generally, work experience in the media consists of short placements (usually two weeks) or work shadowing.

What will I be doing?
It depends which area of the media you are working in. You could be writing short news features in a magazine publishers, acting as a runner for a TV company or looking after guests on a radio show. Be prepared to work without pay, work hard and network your socks off—learn from the professionals around you and find out how they started their own careers.

Tips for applying
It isn't easy getting work experience in the media, but with persistence and an optimistic attitude it is definitely possible. Some of the larger media organisations, such as the BBC and big-name magazine publishers, book work experience placements up to a year in advance; so it's important to be very organised. Application methods vary between different organisations: with some it's best to apply on spec and send in your CV and covering letter; others want you to apply online. Do research on the organisation before you apply. In any application, enthusiasm and interest in the industry is crucial. One of the best ways to show this is by getting involved at university, such as helping to promote Union events, writing for the student paper or working for the university radio station.

WHERE NEXT?

doctorjob.com advice on media and publishing:
doctorjob.com/media
The Bookseller: **www.thebookseller.com**
Media Guardian: **media.guardian.co.uk**
The Publishing Training Centre: **www.train4publishing.co.uk**

MEDICINE

Helping others, making a real difference, excitement and adrenalin, excellent salary . . . there are many reasons why it's good to be a doctor. To be the best, however, you need to know what you want out of life.

Start career planning early so that you have time to understand your skills and motivations and can make a plan of action for meeting your long-term goals. Don't sit back and let others tell you what you should be or do, and don't drift into what seems easiest. Be proactive in seeking out careers guidance, and information and resources provided by your university, medical school, deanery and postgraduate medical centre. Making informed decisions now will help you to shape your future.

No medical degree?

If you haven't got a medical degree, it's not too late to start your career in medicine. You'll have to work hard and be committed, but a fast-track graduate medical degree is your route to joining the medical profession.

Understand all your options

With some 60 specialties and subspecialties, medicine is a profession with a very diverse range of career options. You'll experience some specialties during medical school; others you will be exposed to for the first time during your foundation training—but there will be some that you may never come into contact with unless you seek them out. Make sure you know all your options so that you can match your skills and interests to the right career for you, not forgetting options such as an academic career, working overseas, training in the armed forces.

Stay up to date

Postgraduate medical education is undergoing significant changes at the moment; so it's wise to keep an eye on what's going on. The websites below will help you to stay up to date with the latest information on foundation programmes and postgraduate medical education.

Remember to visit your deanery's website to find out how changes will be implemented in your region and also visit the websites of the medical royal colleges.

Deaneries and training

Deaneries are responsible for managing and delivering postgraduate medical education (PGME) and they oversee appointments to training posts and provide direct support to doctors in training via clinical tutors. PGME is the training a doctor will receive before entering the NHS as a staff grade, consultant or GP.

Pay and benefits

The NHS is the largest employer in Europe. It employs over 1.3 million people and serves over 50 million people in England alone.

A medical graduate in his or her pre-registration year would receive a basic salary and in most cases a banding supplement determined by extra hours and/or out-of-hours worked and work intensity. The most common banding supplement would give a doctor an extra 50 percent of basic salary, but this could mean working up to 56 hours a week. In total, a doctor would typically earn £30,443 in their first year following graduation. Competent individuals who progress through their training could reach consultant status within ten years. All staff employed by the NHS are eligible to join the NHS pension scheme, which offers an excellent package of pension benefits, fully protected against the market and guaranteed by the government.

There are, of course, many more medical career paths you can follow. Have a look at the links below for more ideas.

> **WHERE NEXT?**
>
> doctorjob.com advice on medical careers: **doctorjob.com/medicine**
> General Medical Council (GMC): **www.gmc-uk.org**
> NHS Modernising Medical Careers: **www.mmc.nhs.uk**
> NHS Employers: **www.nhsemployers.org**
> British Medical Association: **www.bma.org.uk**
> Department of Health: **www.dh.gov.uk**
> NHS Careers: **www.nhscareers.nhs.uk**

PR

Public relations (PR), also called 'communications' in some organisations, is about promoting and protecting the reputation and image of an organisation or individual.

The PR industry has a turnover of £6.5 billion in the UK, contributes £3.4 billion to the UK's economic activity and generates £1.1 billion in corporate profits. On a global scale, the UK PR market is second only to that of the US.

Entry routes

Some larger organisations run structured graduate training schemes, but in-house and smaller independent consultancies generally recruit into entry-level PR positions. As a graduate, you may start off as a PR assistant (in-house), or as a PR officer or a junior account executive (agency).

What will I do?

There are a number of areas of overlap, whether you work in-house or for a consultancy. A job in PR will involve a lot of communication, both within your organisation and with external contacts such as media, the public and other organisations. Part of your role will be proactive, but you'll also need to be prepared to react to enquiries and events that can't be anticipated.

Working in PR will involve speaking with people from your organisation and with your clients—after all, you are representing them. You may need to gather information from them, check whether anything newsworthy is happening, and liaise with them on any current publicity.

You may need to make television and radio appearances, or train others in how to do this professionally and effectively. Also, be prepared to be out of the office, and on occasion to work out of office hours, since your role may involve travelling or obligatory after-hours socialising.

WHERE NEXT?

doctorjob.com advice on careers in PR: **doctorjob.com/advertising**
PR Week: **www.prweek.com/uk**

PROPERTY

Property professionals agree: no two days are the same. You'll need a variety of skills, and the people and properties you work with will be equally diverse.

SURVEYING: WHAT'S IT ALL ABOUT?

Buying, selling, leasing, planning, developing, managing, investing . . . surveyors do pretty much anything that can be done with property, which means career opportunities are very diverse—everything from consultancy work to managing a rural estate.

Competition to get into the profession is tough. But once you have your foot on the ladder the opportunities are good, particularly in under-subscribed disciplines such as building surveying, residential and rural practice. If you have the right mix of people skills and professional expertise you'll be able to go far.

If you're looking for a 'City' job with a difference, this career could fit the bill. You'll have the buzz of doing deals, but you are working with a physical product: you can see the properties that you have worked on.

- ✔ **Working hours.** The work–life balance isn't bad—hours are usually from around 8.30 am until 6.30 pm, but you can expect a lot of client functions.
- ✔ **Variety**. You will work on a number of different projects using many different skills.
- ✔ **Professional qualifications.** These bring increased job security, respect and earning potential.
- ✔ **Sociability.** If you consider yourself to be a 'people person' this sector is for you.
- ✔ **Money.** Like any profession, the rewards are good, particularly when you get to the top.

What about the old boys' network?

Membership of the Royal Institution for Chartered Surveyors (RICS) is still dominated by the proverbial white male. But the number of women and ethnic minority surveyors is rising steadily. While female RICS members make up only 11 percent of total membership, the proportion of female trainees is 17 percent, and, when you get to student members, that rises to 23 percent.

What's happening in the profession?

The sector is influenced by both commercial and political developments. Recent changes include new investor interest in residential property; the trend towards 'mixed use' developments; increased demand for affordable housing; the requirements of the Disability Discrimination Act; and a growing emphasis on sustainability issues.

CONSTRUCTION: AN INTRODUCTION

Do you like working with your hands? Do you have an eye for a good design? Do you like buildings? Would you like to be involved in designing or constructing them? The construction and architecture fields could be your ideal career.

Before construction firms are involved in a project, architects provide the initial plans. They can also coordinate building designs as changes manifest themselves throughout a job's duration. Architects consult with owners, planning departments and a number of other interested parties in proposing designs. Architectural practices are no different from firms in any other sector: they can be small, medium or large, though some of the largest employers such as the government, commercial organisations, banks and retail firms now contract work out. However, private developers and smaller organisations now have more opportunities than previously.

Architects, like most professionals in the property arena, can often work unsociable hours, but there is always the possibility of travel and eventually setting up on your own. Short-term contracts are commonplace, though, and you are always at the mercy of an ever-changing market.

The construction industry has adapted to these wavering foundations with a number of developments. Partnering allows a number of firms to work together, bringing a project off with understanding for the needs of various trades. It is created out of rethought contractual structures and fresh attitudes to working with competitors. Another significant change is the private finance initiative (PFI), which allows the private sector to fund public sector developments and be paid through long term investment in the project (such as being paid for services provided on the finished site). It's an industry that now requires a forward-thinking approach (whether you want to be quantity surveyor or construction manager) and not just the ability to use a shovel and cement mixer.

10 REASONS TO CHOOSE A CAREER IN CONSTRUCTION

1   **Diversity.** Around two million people are already employed in the construction industry in the UK, in over 700 different roles.
2   **Lasting legacy.** One of the most rewarding aspects of a career in construction is having something tangible to show for all the hard work that goes into individual projects.
3   **Part of a team.** Construction is all about teamwork as designers, engineers, surveyors, planners and managers all work together to complete a project. You become part of a diverse team of specialists all working to the same goal.
4   **International opportunities.** The global construction industry is huge and offers great opportunities to work overseas. The UK has a well-deserved world-class reputation in design and build and its construction professionals are in demand all over the world.
5   **A thriving industry.** The construction industry in the UK is thriving and is set to get bigger.
6   **Choice of career route.** There is no set path into a career in construction and the industry is flexible enough to allow you to progress throughout your career by gaining further qualifications and experience.

7 **Professional qualifications.** Most of the career areas in construction offer the chance to become professionally qualified and to join one of the professional institutions. This means that your skills and experience are properly recognised.

8 **Good work–life balance.** Construction professionals work hard but the hours allow you time for your friends, family and outside interests.

9 **Contributing to the economy.** Construction is the UK's largest industry, generating revenues of over £1 billion a year. The construction industry is also essential for growth in other sectors such as housing, infrastructure and improvements in public services.

10 **Challenges, satisfaction, excitement and fun.** A career in one of the many roles in construction will provide challenges and satisfaction, but above all it will be exciting and fun.

WHERE NEXT?

doctorjob.com advice on careers in property: **doctorjob.com/property**

Be Constructive: **www.bconstructive.co.uk**

Career Builder: **www.careerbuilder.co.uk**

The Career Engineer: **www.thecareerengineer.com**

Careers in Construction: **www.careersinconstruction.com**

Royal Institute of Chartered Surveyors: **www.rics.org**

RICS searchable database of firms worldwide: **www.ricsfirms.com**

RETAIL

If you've always thought of retail as shelf stacking then think again. You could be missing out on a career that offers intellectual challenges and excellent starting salaries.

Retail is big business—the second largest employer in the UK in fact. This is hardly surprising as it includes everything from haberdashery and homeware to clothes, food and electrical goods, making the list of potential employers practically endless, from Asda to Zara, Boots to Waterstone's. Retailers are looking for switched-on and motivated graduates capable of driving forward the interests of customers and shareholders through inspirational and innovative leadership in many fascinating and diverse roles: retail management, marketing, buying, IT, finance, HR and visual merchandising.

The retail industry has always picked graduates to fill its senior positions, offering starting salaries that range from £19,000 to £37,000. Unlike many industries, however, retail offers early responsibility, with applicants likely to be overseeing a staff of 30 within two years. The graduate training schemes are as broad-ranging as the careers on offer. You could find yourself involved with launching new products, solving supply chain problems or leading new initiatives.

Always at the height of fashion

Whilst the traditional store format may be the dominant image of retail, the progressive world of online retailing, or 'e-tailing', highlights how the sector is diversifying with new technologies. This particular area will entice a new generation of graduates, and the sector as a whole will continue to provide an environment where innovation, hard work and the ability to sell yourself result in terrific earnings potential.

WHERE NEXT?

doctorjob.com advice on retail careers: **doctorjob.com/retail**
Retail Careers: **www.retailcareers.co.uk**
InRetail industry jobsite: **www.inretail.co.uk**

SCIENCE

Among the very diverse range of science careers are pharmacology, clinical and industrial research, product or process development, clothing and textiles, clinical biochemistry, microbiology and forensic science, to name but a few.

We're surrounded by constantly-evolving technology which is fuelled by continual innovation. Whether it's the latest consumer electronics to hit the high street, a high-tech weather satellite system or the most advanced smart polymer, scientists play a vital role from conception and development of a product or process through to final marketing and support. What's more, the skills of scientists, engineers and mathematicians are increasingly in demand in the UK.

Health professions are a key part of the UK economy and take many science graduates each year—as lab technicians, medical physicists, microbiologists, forensic scientists or radiologists, for example. While many of these roles involve specific vocational training, generalist science graduates can also enter this sector, as can those from non-scientific backgrounds, choosing avenues such as sales or IT.

For science graduates, further study is a common way to secure a career path to the top. For a career in research, whether academic or in the commercial arena, a postgraduate degree can often open up better opportunities, as well as letting you enjoy another few years at university!

Your knowledge, rigour and logical approach are your key selling points. However, employers also want to see your softer side. These days you must demonstrate strong communication skills, team-working abilities and business awareness. Why? Because clients and customers are king; moreover, science still thrives on collaboration, and even the lofty heights of scientific research and innovation face commercial pressures.

Science degrees can lead to anything!

Bearing in mind that 40 percent of graduate jobs are open to students with any degree, as a science graduate you can work in sectors as different from your first degree as law, IT and management consulting. All that time spent poring over stats tables or writing reports with a partner will give you a head start in a world in which dedication and attention to detail,

241

as well as numeracy and teamworking skills, are sometimes more important than sector knowledge.

But don't be too quick to leave your degree subject behind. Wouldn't it be nice to use some of your hard-won knowledge in your working life? And don't think that your options will be limited. For example, a microbiologist or biochemist can work as (deep breath) a research scientist, a quality control technician, a dietician, a civil service administrator, a technical sales executive, a teacher, a forensic scientist, a conservation officer or a meteorologist. And that's not all. You can work in a classroom, a lab, an office, out-of-doors or on television. You can work anywhere in the UK or abroad, for a large multinational film or for a local authority.

So, how can you choose which is best for you? Remember that it's not just a case of your technical skills; your soft skills, tastes, personality and where you want to work should all be taken into account. Think about your course and how its particular components have helped you hone certain skills. As a scientist it's more than likely that you will have undertaken a large research project that will have stretched your teamwork, managing and organisational skills—something to call to mind when you're asked by an interviewer to give an example of solving a problem or persuading others.

Having assessed your skills, think carefully about what you want from a job. Would you pine in an office or do you prefer the outdoors? Do you feel most at home in a lab? Do you work well on your own or do you thrive in the company of other people?

WHERE NEXT?

doctorjob.com advice on science careers: **doctorjob.com/science**

Biology Jobs: **www.biologyjobs.co.uk**

Defence Science and Technology Laboratory:
www.dstl.gov.uk/careers/index.php

Jobs in Science, Clinical and Engineering: **www.srg.co.uk**

AAAS Science Careers: **aaas.sciencecareers.org**

New Scientist jobsite: **www.newscientistjobs.com/graduate**

ScienceNet: **www.sciencenet.org.uk/careers/careerindex.html**

TEACHING

A career in teaching offers job satisfaction, great development prospects and the chance to work with amazing individuals.

Wanting to go into teaching is not aspiring to the unattainable, but it does need determination. It is a demanding and sometimes frustrating career that needs to be approached with the eyes wide open in anticipation of some of the realities in store.

The range of positive things available to teachers is enormous, from the intellectual buzz of engaging with motivated and able pupils to the equally genuine thrill of getting some otherwise recalcitrant pupil to acknowledge that the lesson you've painstakingly prepared and finally managed to teach was actually 'quite good'. There's the satisfaction of helping to reshape the departmental scheme of work so that it makes more sense; the fantastic moments at end-of-year ceremonies when you see your beloved group who have driven you mad with their inspired indolence finally spread their wings and go off to the next phase of their lives; the privilege of meeting the parents of particular pupils and finally realising why they are the little angels or devils that confront you every day. Priceless moments all.

✔ **Satisfaction.** Any teacher will tell you that it's the best feeling in the world when a lesson goes well. New challenges come, not just from different lessons, but from the individual personalities of those you teach. It is the students who help to make teaching a unique and fulfilling career.

✔ **Money.** The main reasons cited by teachers for entering the profession are a desire to give something back to the community and a genuine interest in working with children. But altruism doesn't pay the bills, so you'll be pleased to know that since September 2006 the starting salary for newly-qualified teachers in England and Wales has been set at £19,641 (£23,577 in inner London). There's also a comprehensive package of discounts and benefits available.

✔ **Support.** At every stage of your career you will have access to a support network of colleagues, union representatives and organisations such as the Teacher Support Network who can provide a helping hand. In fact in terms of support and career

243

development, teaching is one of the best professions.

✔ **Prospects.** Teaching offers many career development opportunities, whether you want to specialise in a certain aspect of teaching or rise up the ranks of management to become a head teacher. The Fast Track Teaching programme is one way to aim for the top, but there are loads of opportunities for motivated graduates.

Who can apply?

You can! Teachers come from all degree backgrounds and there's no specific teaching 'type'. If you're thinking about a career in teaching (and if you're even vaguely interested, then it's worth finding out more), talk to teachers—their enthusiasm is infectious and you'll get to find out first hand what the work and environment are like.

The general requirement for teaching at a secondary school is to have degree-level knowledge in a national curriculum subject, but this is not a requirement for teaching at primary level. Some course providers will look at your A level results for the subject you wish to teach and take that into consideration.

While your degree subject should support the work you will do as a teacher, it is important to take a broad view. For example, degrees such as engineering or mineralogy may not be on the curriculum, but can still be relevant to subjects such as science or maths. Equally, some schools offer non-national curriculum subjects such as sociology and therefore need teachers with relevant qualifications. If you are unsure as to whether you would be eligible to teach your chosen subject it's a good idea to visit your preferred course provider's website to check their requirements.

Are you ready?

It's essential that you get your bearings before embarking on training. Most important is to ensure that before interview you gain some experience of what schools are like today.

Visit a school for a day or two and see what actually goes on and what pupils are like. Then ask yourself if it's really for you. Bear in mind that training courses are funded by the government to provide teachers for the state system, so the institution where you train will not be apologetic about sending you to an ordinary school. You may also get experience of a relatively 'easy' school, but don't count on it.

Once you've had a look, ask yourself some serious questions. Are you ready for the demands of teaching—the preparation time, the emotional strain of dealing with pupils' personal problems while still keeping a professional distance, the necessity of good time management, the interpersonal skills needed for coping with children and colleagues?

Why do students drop out of teacher training courses?

Teacher training courses take care to enrol students who they expect to go on to successful teaching careers. Naturally, though, a percentage of students leave without completing the course. Bear in mind however that colleges who have enrolled you will generally not want to lose you and sometimes allow a leave of absence—for up to two years in some cases— to give time for issues to be resolved. Reasons for dropping out include:

- ✔ **Personal reasons.** This could range from illness, bereavement or having to move away from the area because partners change jobs. For many students, financial issues can be a factor, especially if they have not planned for the PGCE year's costs.
- ✔ **Changing age range.** Very occasionally students realise through the experience of the course that they would prefer teaching a different age group: for example a secondary course student may decide that primary or post-16 only is more appealing.
- ✔ **Workload.** The postgraduate PGCE route has just over nine months to equip students with what they need to operate as teaching professionals. The intensity of the course, and its challenges on intellectual, physical and emotional levels, can sometimes astound students, especially if they see the course as

an extension of their university studies rather than a professional postgraduate training course.

✔ **Attitude to managing learning.** Most people start the PGCE course with limited experience of managing the learning of a whole group. Many come with a zeal for sharing their learning without realising that they have to motivate pupils' interest, involve them in learning, and not lecture at them or treat them as empty vessels into which to pour information. Some intellectually very able people have huge problems coping with pupils of average ability, never mind those of below average ability.

✔ **Attitude to managing behaviour.** Children require managing, and will not give teachers automatic respect. This causes problems, especially for older students and those from other cultural backgrounds where teachers have natural respect. Some people find it very difficult to act as a manager because their personality is not suited to it.

✔ **Attitude to being a trainee.** Some people on second careers, especially if they've been a manager in their previous career, find coping with the junior role of trainee in a school very difficult, especially if they are being managed/mentored by a younger person. Some men have a cultural difficulty being managed by a woman.

WHERE NEXT? ✔

doctorjob.com advice on teaching careers: **doctorjob.com/teaching**
Fast Track Teaching programme: **www.fasttrackteaching.gov.uk**
Teachernet: **www.teachernet.gov.uk**
Training and Development Agency for Schools (TDA):
www.tda.gov.uk

INDEX